clear & present

a practical guide to authenticity

DAVE WAXLER

NEW CLARITY MEDIA

ISBN 978-1-69-118385-2

1 - INTRODUCTION
CLEAR & PRESENT

When a firefighter runs into a burning building they are facing a situation they have never seen before. We think of them as heroes because they are doing something we ourselves would never do. Some of the most terrifying things most people can imagine they actually do for a living.

In simple terms the job of a firefighter is to take control of a situation that is out of control. What makes this more challenging is that a firefighter never fights the same fire twice. Every emergency has its own set of problems that are uniquely unfamiliar and entirely unpredictable. No matter how much they train they will always find themselves dealing with uncertainty and potentially life threatening risk.

In the midst of danger they don't have time to consult an instruction manual. They have to rely on their instincts and courage and take immediate action. Although they spend years practicing techniques and developing their skills, none of it matters if they don't have the confidence to show up and save lives while protecting themselves and each other from harm.

As a psychotherapist I have spent more than a decade serving people who are experiencing their own emergencies. It may be depression or anxiety, family conflict, grief, anger, or harmful habits, even thoughts of suicide. Sometimes their concerns are uncomfortable but manageable. In other cases they feel like their life is a burning building. In all cases they are approaching a situation they have never seen before and they feel unable to confront alone.

What my clients tell me they want most is answers. Will my marriage survive? Should I quit my job? Why am I depressed? How can I control my anxiety? When will things get better? Over the years I have learned that what they really need is confidence.

The word **confidence** comes from the Latin word **fidelis** which means "faith in something that hasn't yet been seen." When a person is confident they are able to respond to any situation without always knowing what is about to happen. It brings with it a sense of living with uncertainty.

Many of my clients are ashamed and frustrated because they think they should be able to predict and control their lives. What they must learn to accept is that each situation in life has its own set of problems that are uniquely unfamiliar and entirely unpredictable.

We are all first responders in our own life. Even with years of personal growth, learning new skills, and practicing countless techniques, the truth is you will never fight the same fire twice. What really matters is developing the confidence to trust your instincts and respond to the steady flow of change that arises in every moment.

This is what it means to be clear and present. That's what this book is about.

In my work I have done a great deal of research and spent many years learning and consulting with other professionals. I have provided thousands of hours of therapy and crisis interventions to individuals of all ages and backgrounds. The information and strategies in this book have been tried and tested by my clients in their daily lives.

It was written with a sincere desire to begin a dialog about what it's like to live an authentic life. It is intended to be a resource for anyone I happen to have the privilege of serving in my role as a therapist, teacher, and friend. It was born out of a necessity to compile a set of ideas that have been enormously beneficial to my clients in the process of therapy.

Over the years I have looked for ways to understand and communicate a multitude of concepts collected from a wide array of disciplines including psychology, economics, biology, sociology, popular culture and even comedy to explain things in a way that makes them approachable and applicable.

That's why I've made it a point to keep this as simple and practical as possible. It is deliberately concise. Rather than a comprehensive review of research data and theoretical literature I'm convinced that my clients, and you the reader, would prefer a guidebook that introduces new ideas that are realistic and useful.

The concepts are presented in a format that is brief and to the point with exercises that can be easily completed for personal benefit. Whenever possible I've included some references for further exploration on your own. If you are curious or disagree with something you read I encourage you to follow your instincts and do some research to learn more.

At the end of the day this is a **self-help** book. You have to do the work yourself. You have your own story and all of the challenges that come with it. You've learned from your experiences, made your own mistakes, struggled with countless questions and conflicts. You've got your own strongly held beliefs and opinions about how things work. I'm not ignorant to the fact that you will decide how you use this information, apply what works, and discard the rest.

My approach to therapy is collaborative. In order to role model authenticity and integrity for my clients I begin by asking them to tell me when they think I am wrong. In this way we both share responsibility for the outcome of our work together. My hope is that this book will offer the same opportunity for readers to find their own answers and generate as many or more compelling questions.

It should also be noted that this is literally a **self** help book. It is about taking a look at your individual concept of self and working towards a deeper understanding of how that shapes your quality of life. By far one of the most effective strategies I have seen in helping my clients is coaching them on ways to be more reflective and intentional in striving for authenticity.

Although the idea of authenticity has become a popular buzzword its meaning has become somewhat ambiguous in our culture. On the surface it might feel like an excuse to be self-centered or even condescending. The motivation to be authentic may come from a desire to have a more satisfying and meaningful life. Many of my clients are surprised to find out how difficult and even painful it can be to work towards this goal.

This is why confidence is essential in opening up to such a transformative experience. After a lifetime of looking for answers outside of themselves, and sometimes hiding from their inner demons, many of my clients tell me they are apprehensive about beginning the work of self-examination. For those who have encountered significant trauma it can be even more overwhelming.

In order to reassure them I have developed a formula to serve as a framework for where to begin and how to proceed.

CONFIDENCE = CLARITY + CONSISTENCY

When you meet someone it's not uncommon for them to ask what you do. Your answer will typically be a job title or some label that makes it easy for them to categorize you. This may be useful as a social skill but it can be harmful if you allow that description to define you. What you do for a living doesn't always tell the whole story about who you really are.

If you allow yourself to be defined from the outside in you will find it more difficult to genuinely know yourself. In order to live with confidence you must begin by first clarifying WHO you are and let that define WHAT you do and WHY you do it.

With this level of clarity you will be able to devise an effective strategy for living a more authentic life. You can ask yourself, "How does what I do help me become the person I want be?" This is the definition of self-actualization.

There is a saying I use to emphasize this aspect of confidence.

Your role defines your goal.

Very often people find themselves confused about how they should relate to others or respond to their current situation. It's easy to find yourself with competing interests and goals that contradict each other. This will either leave you paralyzed with doubt or overwhelmed with frustration. When you don't know the answer to the question "What should I do?" it might be better to ask instead "Who do I want to be?"

Once you have a clear understanding of who you are and how that defines your role and goals, you have still only solved half of the equation. In order to maximize the benefits of confidence it's essential to learn how to measure the results of your actions to improve your consistency over time.

Fundamentally there are two ways to measure consistency. You should measure both the **quality** of your actions (how well you do them), and the **quantity** of your actions (how often you do them).

By clarifying what actions will help you be more authentic, and then measuring how consistently you do them, you are engaging in a much higher level of effort than most people have ever even considered. Remember that the more specifically you make plans the more likely they are to happen.

The best part about this process is that it works even when you make mistakes. Because you are paying attention to the results of your actions you will at least know why you aren't getting the results you want. True confidence is knowing what to do, even when you don't know what you are doing. There is another saying that helps with this part of the equation.

Focus on direction not perfection.

Believing that you will somehow complete this process is a recipe for endless frustration and disappointment. Growth is a response to change, and change is the reason for growth. They go hand in hand. Authentic confidence is the surest evidence of your ability to adapt to unpredictable change and thrive in a dynamic and sometimes dangerous world.

In the following chapters you will explore the link between confidence and authenticity. They are presented in a particular order because they build on each other towards a complete picture of the ingredients of an authentic life.

In chapter two you will identify **Authentic Values**. The search for authenticity must inherently begin from the inside out shining a light on the complicated connection between the image you portray to the world and the way you imagine our inner self.

In chapter three you will examine **Authentic Emotions**. By recognizing the critical need for resiliency you will become more willing to accept and even appreciate the challenges that occur as you strive for a life of integrity.

In chapter four you will learn about **Authentic Intentions**. A strategic journey into the causes and effects of disillusionment will help you set more practical goals and elevate the universal search for meaning in your life.

In chapter five you will consider the importance of **Authentic Relationships**. With a blend of classic psychology and modern science you will uncover new insights into the purpose of conflict in teaching you about yourself.

In chapter six you will reflect on some important concepts about **Authentic Living**. Building on your own instinctive need for play as a tool for healing and growth you can create an outlook that cultivates a lifestyle that is more fulfilling and genuinely authentic.

At the end of these chapters there is a summary of the key points and questions you can use to journal or discuss with others.

In chapter seven you will find a series of exercises on **Authentic Thinking** that can be used to gain further insight on ways to apply these concepts in your daily life.

If you are using this book for personal development it would be ideal as a resource to collaborate with your own therapist. If you are a mental health practitioner or serving as a mentor you may find the questions at the end of each chapter and the exercises to be a useful tool in guiding those who look to you for support.

If you are experiencing a crisis or serious mental illness you should consult a mental health practitioner in addition to this material. This book has been written for educational purposes only. The ideas and exercises provided are not intended to be a replacement for professional mental health services.

I should also mention that all of the comments and stories about clients in this book have been altered to protect their privacy. Any discussion about personal information is merely anecdotal and intended only to illustrate key points of interest, and to help readers connect with the concepts in an authentic way.

It is my hope that these ideas can inform and inspire you in the same way I have seen them help so many others in my practice.

2 - AUTHENTIC VALUES
BEHIND THE MASK

Ancient Greek actors would appear in an amphitheater to entertain the crowd. Because it was a few thousand years ago they obviously didn't have modern technology like cameras and microphones, so they invented ways to help a large audience enjoy the experience.

The amphitheater itself was shaped like a bowl to hold as many people as possible and was designed to amplify sound from the bottom to the very top. In order to be seen the masks that the actors used were larger than life. They were sometimes as big as the actor themselves and had a built in megaphone much like the ones used by cheerleaders today. The actor would speak through the megaphone so their voice could be heard as they stood behind their giant mask.

The Greek word for mask is **persona** which means "sounding through." Each mask was used to represent a particular character in a play. Sometimes there were even different versions of the character's persona to indicate a change of mood. This is where we get the modern idea of a personality.

When we talk about someone's personality it's not uncommon to discuss certain aspects of their *character*. We typically say someone is *acting* a certain way and sometimes they are being *dramatic*. These are all references to this idea that who we are is somehow hidden behind a mask.

This is a familiar concept that we accept as a normal part of life. A mask is a convenient tool to hide the flaws and insecurities we have collected over the course of our lives. The problem occurs when we begin to rely on the mask so much that we can't imagine living without it.

On the outside we appear perfectly fine, participating in the drama and saying our lines, taking a bow when the show is over. But on the inside we feel exhausted from the effort of entertaining a crowd of spectators, uncertain if we can ever be appreciated for who we truly are.

The thought of taking off the mask and exposing our true self can seem intolerable. What's even worse is when we can't tell the difference between the mask and our true identity. We can become so dependent on the mask that it begins to define us. The mask becomes a permanent fixture and our real self becomes neglected and malignant.

A great deal of my work has to do with learning more about the self and the concept that humans develop about the person they think they are. Over the last decade I've spent a lot of time meeting with individuals and families in crisis. This has given me an opportunity to hear countless stories about the challenges people face, and their hope for a better life.

In order to create lasting improvements a person must redefine who they think they are rather than just how they behave.

They often tell me stories of trauma, severe family conflict, addictions, disorders, disease, loss and grief. Many people who want to give up are plagued with shame about what has happened to them, or what they have done. Others are angry about the abuse they have endured and the possibility of a better life that was stolen from them. So much of their identity has been defined for them from the outside in. Who they are feels like a prison sentence. They long to be free from the mask they wear to hide their pain and insecurity.

I often hear them say they just can't live with themselves, or they have been finding ways to harm themselves, or that they even want to kill themselves. All of these problems are related to the idea that their sense of self is to blame. They have come to believe that without the mask they are a person who is unworthy of acceptance and love. Many times they are overwhelmed by their circumstances, sometimes by their own self destructive choices, but many more times by events that are completely out of their control.

Someone struggling with suicidal thoughts once told me that she didn't really want to die, she just wanted to start over. This feeling of despair represents a crisis that many people face when they believe they have nothing left to lose. It is at this point that they have run out of hope, and that may sound like a bad thing. But in my work it can become a perfect opportunity.

If the problem is related to an intolerable self, how can we work to accept the self so that a person can remove the mask without fear? What is it about the hidden self that is so unacceptable? How can we rehabilitate their wounded identity so that a person can live a life on their own terms? How can someone nurture an authentic self, unique and empowered to be who they want to be?

The word **authentic** means "true to itself." When we talk about a document, or a piece of art being authentic, we mean that the thing being described has its own identity and is not a copy of something else. Authenticity comes from the same place where we get the word **author**. It's a word that describes someone who gets to decide who they want to be on their own; a person who gets to write their own story.

The search for authenticity begins with the process of looking behind the mask you use to cover up the self on the inside. Many people I work with have come to the conclusion that doing so is too painful to bear. They may be afraid to accept who they really are, unable to imagine a self that isn't so intolerable.

Finding Our "Self"

Change itself is not really a good thing or a bad thing. It's how you respond to change that makes a huge difference in your mental health. When you are dealing with grief, anxiety, depression, and many other mental illnesses, the underlying cause is often a failure to feel a sense of control over what is happening to you and around you. The unpredictable nature of existence can cause you to doubt your own ability to make sense of the past or face an uncertain future.

Burdened with self-doubt, you may find it harder and harder to trust yourself to make good decisions. You may interpret the normal challenges of life as a result of weakness and begin to live in shame. Your relationships might become confrontational and exhausting. It doesn't take long before you can begin to lose track of your values and begin to feel like your life lacks purpose and direction.

On the contrary, when you have a healthy sense of self you are capable of clarifying your own values and using them to set balanced and meaningful goals. Your relationships are affirming and fulfilling. You can embrace change as a fact of life and work consistently toward self-improvement.

The evidence is very clear that the best way to turn the tide of mental illness is to begin to heal the self. Research shows that changes in behavior and outlook are far more likely to last when a person changes how they see themselves.[1]

If a you want to lose weight you may decide to go to the gym and eat a healthy diet. These actions may be effective in the short term but over time they are likely to drop off when you are distracted by other activities or can't find the motivation to keep going.

In order to create lasting improvements you must redefine who you think you are rather than just how you behave. If you work towards seeing yourself as a healthy person who makes healthy choices it will become part of your identity. It begins to infiltrate every part of your life. Your motivations build on each other so that your healthy choices are more rewarding and fulfilling.

Not only are you going to the gym, but you might also go to bed earlier or begin to hang out with other healthy people. You begin to feel good about who you are so that every healthy choice doesn't just improve your body, but plays a role in the larger goal of reinforcing your sense of self.[2]

As a therapist I have become keenly aware of how a person's self-image can affect their ability to heal and grow. If you see yourself as inherently flawed you have little chance of making improvements because you are defeated before you even begin. All of your hard work feels like a waste of time. If you can learn to see yourself as capable and resilient you can overcome many emotional barriers to making better choices.

On the day you are born you begin the process of learning who you are. What may be the biggest identity crisis of all is emerging from the womb as a separate human being. You are literally cut off from your mother to become a new person. The story of child development is really a story about becoming a unique individual.

For the first few years of childhood you are working on gaining control of your body, and then your environment. You learn to walk, talk, explore and eventually make your own decisions about what you want to do and how you want to do it.

We are all familiar with toddlers wanting to do things for themselves. This typically leads to some amount of frustration and a few messes along the way. As you grow older from childhood into adolescence you are following a well-worn path toward self-sufficiency and independence. This journey is filled with countless difficulties that come from carving out an identity that feels right.

So much of who you are is defined for you before you even have a chance to know yourself. You are born into a family you didn't choose surrounded by people who tell you who you are including your gender, ethnicity, culture, and beliefs. You are taught to speak and behave according to a set of rules defined by many different authority figures. Nearly every aspect of your "self" is influenced by the world around you.

By the time you reach adolescence you develop the cognitive abilities to question this external influence. What is sometimes seen as rebellion is really part of a normal and necessary process of reclaiming ownership of your identity.

In a healthy adult this process leads to a secure and stable sense of self with clear values and the confidence to live with integrity. If this process is interrupted or delayed it can create unresolved problems that prevent you from living your values in the right direction.

Imagine a wheel with a central hub held together by multiple handles used to steer a massive ship. The center of the wheel is your sense of self and the handles are the relationships that influence you on a daily basis. The spokes of the steering wheel are the values that those relationships impose on your self-image.

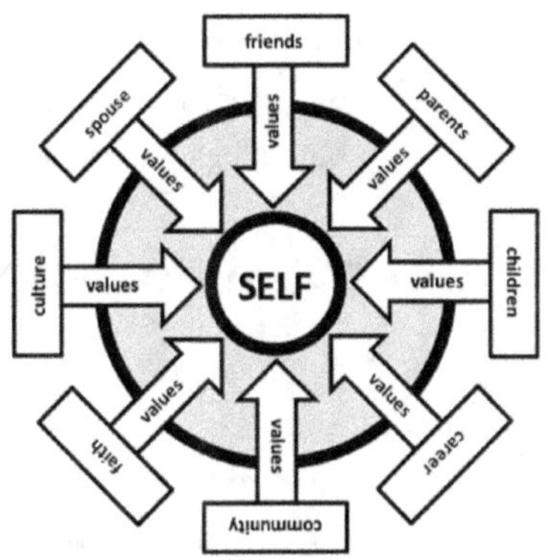

In this arrangement every relationship has a different set of rules. As the person in the middle you have to reimagine who you are with each relationship you encounter. This can cause you to feel infinitely confused and frustrated. Then as each relationship evolves, each set of rules will change leaving you with a constant state of uncertainty about how to act and who you are.

Whenever you try to steer the ship, every relationship pulls you in a different direction. You are constantly trying to compensate for other people's shifting values. In order to make one relationship work you may have to upset the expectations of everybody else. Over time you may feel lost and discouraged because so much effort is spent getting nowhere, feeling out of control.

In an authentic life you decide for yourself what values you will apply to the relationships around you. Your values come from the inside out and create a much more consistent set of rules about how you will respond to the expectations of others. As a result you have a clear sense of who you are.

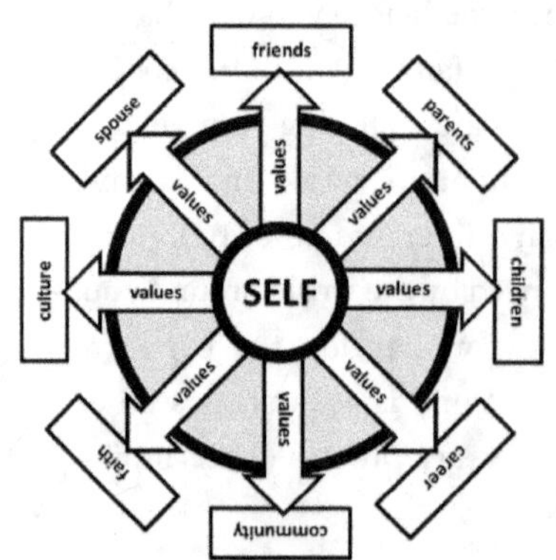

When you try to steer the ship you are able to focus your energy toward a clear goal and move in a certain direction. If you find yourself headed off track it is easier to make corrections because you only have to make adjustments to one set of rules about how you want to live.[3]

Instead of having to make constant adjustments to your self-image, you approach each conflict with a consistent set of values that inform you about how you need to live. Because you know yourself better you can be confident that no matter what happens in the future you are clear about what values will matter to you when you get there.

Integrity Is Expensive

When engineers build a bridge they design it with one thing in mind. Regardless of how beautiful it may be the most important aspect of the structure is its ability to stand up to the pressure it is meant to endure. How much weight will it bear? How long will it last? How well can it perform over time? This is what they are talking about when they use the term structural integrity.

If we were to look at your own integrity we would likely consider the same things. How much weight can you withstand when you are tested? What will you do when things get tough? How well can you respond to challenges that come your way?

That's the thing about integrity. You can talk about it all day long but the truth will be obvious when you encounter the difficulties and burdens of life. If you really want to know if you have integrity it has to cost you something. You will likely have to suffer before you know how much you are able to bear.

Sadly, you might think that your difficulties are a sign of weakness. You might see your suffering as some sort of condemnation about who you are. When bad things happen you can be tempted to tell yourself you have done something wrong. This could make you think your integrity is in question. Maybe it's your fault. Maybe you screwed up.

Thinking like this can only lead to further difficulty. It can easily cause you to consider abandoning your values and give in to the pressure. This is the opposite of what needs to happen.

The truth is a crisis not only demands your integrity but can verify it at the same time. When things get tough, that's when you get to really see who you are on the inside. The structure of your character matters. Sure you may look good on the outside when everything is going your way. But when the weight of the world starts to pile up all the pretty paint and decorations on the bridge have no real meaning. What really matters is what's underneath.

The reason that suffering happens is not in spite of your values, but because of them. The things that bother you are really a clear indicator of the things you care about. It's your integrity that keeps you holding on to these values even when the going gets tough. That's why they call them values in the first place. They are the things in life you have decided are worth something. They will cost you if you want to make them a reality.

If you didn't care about something it wouldn't bother you and you would have no trouble letting go. More often than not when you are struggling with what to do in a certain situation it's because you have two conflicting values that are competing with each other.

A mother who wants to work in order to provide for her family also wants to be home with them. These are two very positive motivations. Both are valuable to her and so they both cost her something. Choosing one over the other requires a great deal of integrity. This crisis is not a sign of her weakness or inadequacy. It is in fact because of her integrity that it bothers her at all.

There may be a student who wants to explore his creativity and pursue a career in art. Meanwhile his parents want him to study science so he can have a more stable career. He is worried that he will upset them but he doesn't want to regret postponing his dreams. Regardless of his decision he knows he will have to face some level of difficulty. In the end whatever decision he makes will serve to verify the cost of his integrity.

So much of the mental and emotional pain you face is more about making your decisions than living with them. Many of my clients are relieved to discover that that their crisis is not about WHO they are but HOW they are. Once you accept the cost of your integrity the real challenge is learning how to clarify your values and recalibrating your life to live more authentically.

Over time you can begin to trust yourself again. You can more readily accept your limitations and avoid the shame and blame that holds you back. When you do make mistakes you can learn from them without feeling like a failure. You will recognize a greater confidence about making decisions, and feel less anxious about the discomfort of change.

The Costs and Benefits of Authenticity

As we mentioned before choosing to work towards authenticity will likely lead to some dramatic changes in your sense of self and in the relationships around you. It might mean you will lose some friends or change your relationship with a family member, or a coworker who is used to you acting in a certain way.[4] At the same time it may create opportunities for new relationships that you could not have previously considered or make some current relationships become more meaningful and fulfilling.

Over the years I have coached clients in making changes in their thinking in order to act more authentically in their lives. Many of them have reported becoming aware of some unexpected differences in themselves and how they respond to challenges in their lives. Here is a list of some of the costs and benefits some have reported as they choose to live a more authentic life.

The Costs of Authenticity

Discomfort – Any time you make changes you will experience discomfort. Of course change is happening all the time and so discomfort is a part of your life as well. When you choose to live authentically you are bound to experience some growing pains that come with the territory.

Remind yourself that living without authenticity is also uncomfortable and gets you nothing in return. Becoming true to yourself means you will need to take some managed risks in order to experience the benefits.

Conflict – In order to live a more authentic life you will probably begin to make different choices about how to respond to the people around you. Chances are those people have come to expect certain behaviors from you, and they may be surprised when you don't meet those expectations. This will inevitably lead to conflict and frustration from people who want you to act the way you used to. They may think it's easier for them to change you than to change themselves. Use this experience to identify people you have been rescuing from their own unhealthy patterns. The conflict caused by your authenticity is the best way to help you both live a more satisfying life.

Uncertainty – If you have lived a long time not knowing who you really are, the idea of doing something different can be overwhelming and scary. Stepping into a more authentic life may lead to many uncertain situations and very unfamiliar feelings. This is especially true if you are recovering from trauma or a history of abuse. Give yourself permission to take it as slow as needed and set small achievable goals toward authenticity. A bunch of tiny successes can lead to a much greater level of confidence and help maintain motivation over time.

Grief – The practice of self-examination often leads to deep questions about the past. Once you begin to give up old patterns you may feel a sense of loss about the time you have spent living a life that was unfulfilling or painful. You may also find yourself missing the comfort of unhealthy habits and relationships that are fading away. Allow yourself to process the symptoms of grief— anger, denial, bargaining, depression and acceptance— as you manage the changes you are seeing in your life.

Crisis – Mental health is not an isolated part of your life. Many people struggle with multiple issues that overlap including social, physical, financial and cultural challenges that affect a person's ability to improve their mental health. The search for authenticity will impact every part of your life and could lead to a significant crisis for yourself and your family. This may present difficulties you cannot face alone. You should expect to develop a support system of trustworthy friends and professionals who can assist you in building coping skills and effective strategies for change. If you are already experiencing severe mental illness you should maintain your current treatment and only make changes while consulting with a qualified mental health practitioner.

The Benefits of Authenticity

Confidence – Among the first benefits of authenticity is a renewed sense of confidence that comes from a clarity about yourself and your values. This will lead to a more effective use of time and energy as you learn to streamline your goals and focus on things that matter to you most. You will find it easier to let go of plans that don't align with your integrity and people who are unable to accept or appreciate your true self. As a result, your efforts will feel more meaningful and satisfying while you continue to strive for an authentic life.

Resiliency – By intentionally examining and refining your priorities you will feel more capable of facing challenges that arise in the future. Once you begin to anticipate and embrace the discomfort of change you can develop a sense of resiliency to recover from the storms of life. You will begin to recognize that those experiences not only make you stronger but offer priceless insight into your values to validate your authentic self.

Wholeness – Coming to terms with your inner self requires a great deal of courage. When you live authentically you must accept the unpleasant aspects of your personality, and find a way to embrace them as essential to your identity. In your search for authenticity you will get better at using this insight as a force of creativity and empowerment in nurturing a sense of wholeness and balance in your life. You will become more comfortable with your own idiosyncrasies and better understand why other people bother you as well.

Forgiveness – You may become aware of your bitterness towards those who have harmed you leading to misguided and unnecessary suffering. As hard as it is to let go of the pain, your unwillingness to forgive actually squanders precious time and energy that could be spent on your own healing and growth. In truth you will only be able to forgive others once you learn to forgive yourself. By becoming more authentic you are able to recognize and embrace your own imperfections so you can begin to unravel the web of resentment that distracts you from more meaningful endeavors.

Impact – It's impossible to comprehend the ripple effect of living a more authentic life. Every change you make towards living with integrity has an impact on the lives of others. Some will be offended by your authenticity. Others will be inspired by it. Regardless, the result will always lead to a better outcome for everyone when you are true to yourself. Anything other than authenticity is essentially a form of deception. When you choose to live with authentic values you make it possible for everyone around you to decide how they will respond. In this way you will repel those who cannot accept the real you, and attract the people who can truly appreciate and support your authentic self.

Finding The Real Thing

Lately there's been a lot of talk about how to spot things that are fake. Our world is flooded with concerns about fake news, computer generated images, and artificial intelligence that almost perfectly replicates reality. So much phony information can really make us doubt our ability to find the real thing.

This is even more true when you set out to find your authentic self. It's not uncommon to begin this process with a sense of confusion. Few people instinctively make a deep assessment of their values to an extent that they can identify, much less verbalize, what they truly believe about themselves. And yet that is exactly what is needed in order to effectively shape your own reality.

So you may be asking, "Where do I begin?" The answer is to start with the real thing. Whenever any expert is asked to determine if an object is authentic they must always begin with something else that they already know is authentic. That's how they became an expert; by studying the real thing.

If an art expert is asked to identify a forgery they compare it to all of the other paintings by the same artist. If a bank teller is asked to spot a counterfeit bill they compare it to a bill that they know is legitimate. Both of these experts have spent so much time with the real thing that when a fake comes along it stands out among the rest, and they usually have no trouble rejecting it.

This is the same process you must begin if you are going to be confident in your authenticity. The work you must do is primarily on recognizing those aspects of your character that genuinely define you. You may be tempted to look at what others are doing or listening to feedback from people who think they know what you need. But you will find that this information is rarely helpful if haven't already learned to listen to your own voice.

As you increase your authenticity you will begin to trust your intuition when you encounter tough decisions about your values. If you are new to this you will probably find this uncomfortable and maybe even a bit terrifying. This is especially true if you are being asked to make a decision that causes someone else to suffer in some way.

A woman may be asked to move in with her partner but something tells her she's not ready. Her partner may be pressuring her, but the woman is aware that she will have to give up her independence. In order to be authentic she may risk losing the relationship by declining the offer. But giving in will cost her a priceless sense of self-respect and anxiety about the outcome. Furthermore it will reinforce her insecurity and prolong the process of learning to trust her inner voice. This situation is a perfect opportunity to recognize that the relationship may not be right for her after all.

As you increase your authenticity you will begin to trust your own intuition when you encounter tough decisions about your values.

A man may be driven to build a career that seems lucrative and fulfilling, but very soon he begins to realize that it has a dark side. His business depends on resources that take advantage of low income workers. Although he doesn't ever see the people he is harming, he knows that his own paycheck is essentially coming from their pockets. He could convince himself that he is somehow not responsible since the practice is common in his industry and no one will blame him for doing the same. But the cost of his willful ignorance is in stark contrast to his sense of integrity and this choice is an important milestone in his journey toward an authentic life.

There is a good chance as you read this you are remembering similar situations in your own life. You are not alone in your struggle to find authenticity in a complicated and confusing world. Let me encourage you to recognize the value of this struggle.

Finding your authentic self may feel like an enormous challenge. And that might be true if you are unable or unwilling to look behind the mask that protects you from the outside world. Remember though that the mask you wear is something you invented all by yourself. It is made from all the pieces of yourself that you want the world to see. It isn't necessarily a bad thing, but it is by design an impersonation of who you really are.[5]

Behind the mask are all of the pieces of your identity that you choose not to show to the world, or even yourself. These are the subconscious thoughts, feelings, and aspects of your personality that are hidden, or intolerable, or even downright scary. It is the part you keep in the shadow and rarely ever choose to let out.

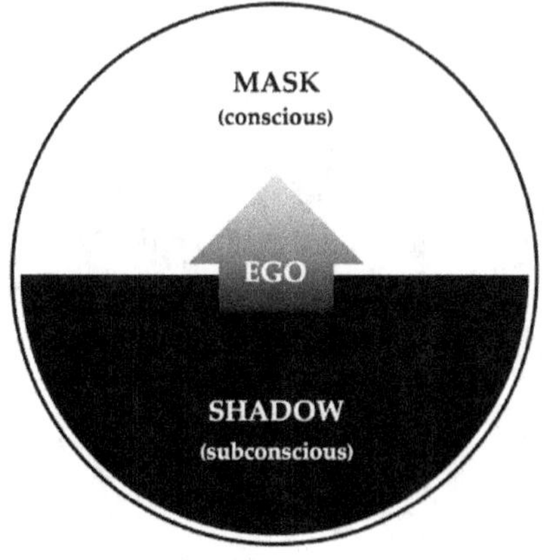

In this framework your mental health is closely related to your ability to regulate the balance between the conscious and subconscious. The work of authenticity is about fine tuning the ego that acts as a doorway between these dual aspects of your identity. Both the conscious and subconscious contrast with each other in a way that defines a person's values.

How can you decide what is good unless you also consider what is bad? How can right and wrong exist without each other? How can you decide if you belong to a group unless you decide who doesn't belong? As long as these questions have clear answers you can feel confident about who you are and how to live your life.

In my work this is rarely the case. Much of the toil in therapy comes from addressing some deeply held insecurities that arise from unresolved conflicts about a person's identity. When the balance between the shadow and the mask is upset it is common for those hidden character traits to sneak out in unhealthy ways.

A girl who experienced body shaming may grow into woman with an eating disorder. A boy who wasn't allowed to be emotionally sensitive may turn into a man with uncontrolled anger. Perfectionists who are afraid of failure may subconsciously be seeking unconditional love. Procrastinators who struggle with motivation may actually feel like imposters unworthy of success. Behaviors that would otherwise be healthy in moderation may evolve into compulsive obsessions that are harmful and out of control.[6]

Exploring the shadow and coming to terms with your own repressed insecurities may turn out to be the most painful part of your search for authenticity. Because of this it may also be the most rewarding. Many people find the process inspires them to be significantly more creative and expressive as they struggle through the pain of self-reflection.

Indeed the conflict between the conscious and subconscious has been fertile ground for nearly every important masterpiece throughout the centuries. From the Greek amphitheater to the modern movie screen we see the same story told in a million different ways.[7]

All the world's a stage, and all the men and women are merely players. It is essential to the human experience to reconcile the internal conflict between the mask you wear and the desire to live a truly authentic life.

CHAPTER 2 NOTES

[1] Duckworth, A. L., Peterson, C., Matthews, M. D., & Kelly, D. R. (January 01, 2007). Grit: perseverance and passion for long-term goals. *Journal of Personality and Social Psychology, 92,* 6, 1087-101.

[2] Reyes, N. R., Oliver, T. L., Klotz, A. A., LaGrotte, C. A., Vander, V. S. S., Virus, A., Bailer, B. A., ... Foster, G. D. (January 01, 2012). Similarities and Differences between Weight Loss Maintainers and Regainers: A Qualitative Analysis. *Journal- Academy of Nutrition and Dietetics, 112,* 4, 499-505.

[3] Beattie, M. (1987). Codependent No More ; How to Stop Controlling Others and Start Caring for Yourself. Harper.

[4] Lerner, H. G. (1989). The dance of anger: A woman's guide to changing the patterns of intimate relationships. New York: Perennial Library.

[5] Jung, C.G. (1938). "Psychology and Religion." In CW 11: *Psychology and Religion: West and East.* p. 131

[6] Chopra, D., Ford, D., & Williamson, M. (2011). *The shadow effect: Illuminating the hidden power of your true self.* New York: HarperOne.

[7] Campbell, J. (1949). *The Hero with a thousand faces.* New York: Pantheon Books

Summary

- Authenticity begins with the process of exploring aspects of your personality that you are unwilling or unable to accept or appreciate.

- Confidence can be strengthened from the inside out by clarifying values and living with integrity.

- Working toward an authentic life requires a certain amount of struggle that often leads to internal conflict and disrupted relationships.

- The benefits of authenticity include a greater sense of resiliency and trust in your own intuition.

Reflections

1. In what ways can wearing a mask be harmful or beneficial?

2. How did your own emotional and intellectual development impact your sense of self?

3. What are some rules that sometimes change depending on the relationship? Which rules need to stay the same no matter what?

4. What are some times in your life when your integrity required you to pay a price that felt right even when it was difficult?

5. How would you rate your ability to recognize your own inner voice? What can you tell yourself to feel more confident?

3 - AUTHENTIC EMOTIONS
BUILDING RESILIENCY

In my work with at-risk youth I was aware that children could not choose the environment they were born into and had no control over the conditions in which they were raised. The challenge was helping children in poverty with dysfunctional families and painfully limited access to resources thrive in a situation where any chance of a better life was dreadfully against the odds. Without intervention their outcome looked bleak.

But what could be done? The research shows that the more adverse childhood experiences that occur in the life of a child the more likely they are to exhibit unhealthy patterns in adulthood. These impacts, known as ACE's, include abuse and neglect, exposure to domestic violence and substance abuse, parental divorce, incarceration, and a family history of mental illness.[8]

A few decades ago, as social workers began to study children who grew up in difficult situations they recognized that although many of these children later exhibited risky and destructive behaviors such as criminal activity, substance abuse, and poor health, a significant number of these kids avoided those same outcomes.

How was it possible for a certain number of children to live in these same conditions facing all of the same challenges as the other kids and come out with very different results? In fact some of these kids not only endured, they excelled ahead of other children with fewer risk factors.

What was the secret?

As researchers studied these situations they developed the concept of **resiliency** to explain how children who are exposed to adverse conditions can survive and even thrive to become healthy adults. Even though we would love to protect children from all the bad things that could happen to them that's not very practical and in truth it's not really what they need.

The children who showed resiliency were the ones who had the support of healthy adults offering unconditional love and high expectations. They had positive role models who had already confronted adversity and represented what success could look like. Instead of removing those children from the environment, their mentors gave them the encouragement they needed to overcome their situation and persist.

Authentic emotions require that same type of resiliency. This idea is not just for children. It's a concept you can use to become more authentic as you deal with challenges that come your way. It is not gained by avoiding discomfort. It comes from facing adversity head on and using it to gain clarity and confidence.

Over time a tree may face many storms and might even lose a few branches. But resilient trees are able to bend in the wind and not break. That's what you are looking for. Although storms cannot be avoided they are a part of life that gives you opportunities for growth.

A crucial step in becoming more authentic is examining the process your own body uses to help you weather the storms of emotion. You may assume that emotional storms mean you are doing something wrong. You might become afraid of your emotions and try to avoid them because they are painful and confusing.

But the human brain has a built-in strategy to remain healthy in the midst of daily storms and even trauma. By becoming aware of the **emotional immune system** you can understand and even appreciate the underlying reasons for feelings of anger, depression, anxiety and shame.

Getting Better

When you get the flu you know you are in for a battle. The symptoms of the flu are pretty familiar. Usually it begins with an itchy throat or runny nose that leads to sneezing and coughing. Not long after that you start to have a fever, or an achy feeling that takes over your body.

Fatigue may set in and maybe even some nausea.

Overall it feels pretty bad. Most of the time you have no choice but to take some time off and wait it out in order to get better. You can treat the symptoms, get plenty of rest, and make sure you take care of yourself. But you know from experience that the real work is going on inside your body.

Your immune system is a miraculous biological defense mechanism. It has evolved over millions of years to respond to foreign invaders that can damage and even destroy your body. It fights off germs, viruses, allergens and many other malfunctions that would otherwise lead to death. And each time it overcomes a pathogen it stores biological information so that it can defeat the enemy the next time it comes around.

You usually take this process for granted, not realizing most of the time that it is working in the background keeping you safe and building up your defenses. It is only when your immune system gets pushed to the limit that you sometimes need to ask for help from a doctor. If the symptoms get too unbearable you may need medicine or surgery to manage the illness.

This process is not only normal, it's also natural and necessary for survival. Challenging your immune system is essential to grow and mature into a healthy functional adult. It's the foundation of all health, not just for fighting off illness and infection, but for strengthening bones, building muscles, and refining your nervous system.

In the same way that human bodies overcome physical challenges from the environment, you have the ability to overcome psychological challenges as well.

With this in mind you can begin to see that healing and illness are basically the same thing. The process of "getting better" is not pretty. The work that a human body must go through to fight off a virus or kill some germs is generally unpleasant and sometimes actually pretty gross.

So when a person gets a physical illness there is no sense of shame or judgement. Since we have all been there ourselves we understand how they feel. We can see someone who is sick and recognize that they are simply doing what it takes to get better.

The same is true of mental illness. Not only do you have a biological immune system, you are also equipped with a remarkably advanced emotional immune system. In much the same way that human bodies overcome physical challenges from the environment, you have the ability to overcome psychological challenges as well.

We often see the brain as separate from the rest of the body because it feels like it does something different than the other organs. Just like the stomach is part of the digestive system, and the lungs are part of the respiratory system, the brain is part of the nervous system. All of these systems are integrated together to function as a single living thing.

At the end of the day the brain's job is to keep you from dying. That's it. Everything it does has something to do with survival. Obviously neurologists have a much deeper understanding of the human brain. But for our purposes we will simplify our discussion by saying that the emotional immune system is built around three main components.

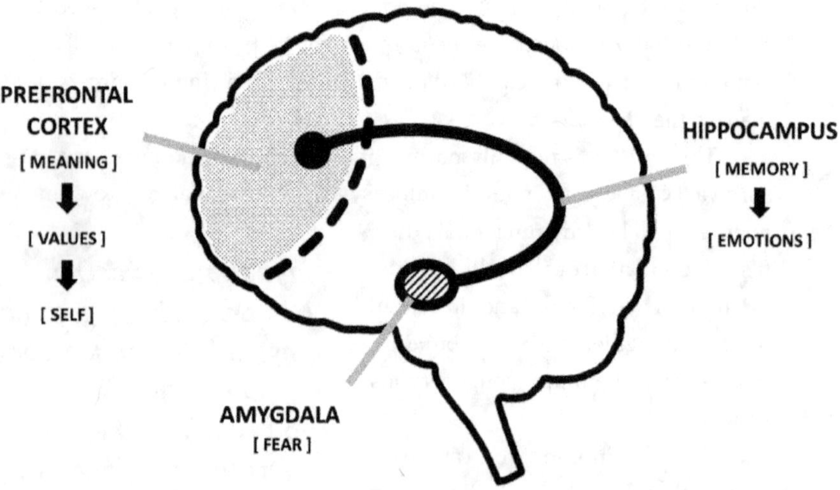

Amygdala - The amygdala is a small collection of neurons on the bottom of your brain about the size of an almond that collects information and makes decisions about threats in the environment. In many ways it is the most primitive part of your emotional immune system and that's why its location is so important.

It is situated right between your ears and right behind your eyes, close to your cerebellum which controls movement through the spinal cord. From here it can pick up sights and sounds that might indicate danger and immediately send signals to your body to fight or run away.

Because it is possibly a life or death situation, it doesn't bother to consult the rest of your brain. It simply responds to the situation before you even know what has happened. This is what you feel when you hear a loud noise and duck your head, or when on object flies toward you and you turn away. In an instant you have an involuntary reaction to protect yourself without having to think about it. This reaction typically comes with a surge of adrenaline and increased heart rate making you pay attention to insure that the threat has been removed. If not, it will continue until you feel safe.

Hippocampus - After the threat has been realized the hippocampus plays a role in collecting data from the experience and turning it into memory. It is a thin structure connected on one end to the amygdala and running though the center of your brain toward your frontal lobe.

During a fearful experience it collects information from all of the senses including sight, sound, smell, touch, and taste. The more threatening an experience appears to be the more information the hippocampus will collect, similar to a high speed camera taking more pictures per second. This is why emotional experiences are more memorable and why recovery from trauma can be so difficult.

Though not as primitive as the amygdala, it tends to be somewhat disorganized and unstructured in thinking. It can be thought of as the subconscious part of the brain since almost all of this activity is happening in the background of your thoughts..

Prefrontal Cortex - Once all of the data has been collected and your emotions are processed, the experience is stored in your prefrontal cortex located at the front of the brain. In simple terms this could be considered the library of your brain because it is the place where all of your experiences are collected to decide what they all mean about your values and in turn about your sense of self.

This is the part of the brain that looks for patterns, problems, and possibilities to help improve decision making and increase your chances of survival. It is the most sophisticated part of your brain and a lot of what it does feels like it is happening under your control. That's why you usually think of this part of your brain as your consciousness.

Scientists looking for the center of consciousness have located a specific part of the prefrontal cortex associated with identity. With precise tools they can stimulate a set of neurons causing a person to temporarily lose their own identity[9] and report a sense of unity with the universe [10]. With this in mind you can gain a new idea about who you are. It's common to approach your sense of self with a great deal of mystery and complexity. But in simple terms your "self" is essentially a lifelong collection of experiences held together by a constant process of deciding what they mean.

Solving the Problem of Self

These three basic components of the brain work together to bolster your defenses against threats, both real and imagined, throughout your life. As you grow older your understanding changes about what constitutes a real threat.

As a newborn infant experiencing hunger you may have been convinced that you were on the brink of starvation. It quite literally felt like a life threatening situation and as a result you cried out for someone to feed you. As soon as food arrived you began to learn that your fear of starvation might have been a little exaggerated, and having successfully overcome the problem, you had a better idea about how to resolve it in the future.

This is a basic example of an emotional immune response. A threat is realized, the challenge is faced, and the resolution brings about new understanding. Over time your fear of starvation has become less threatening and you are now more resilient than before.

It should be noted that resiliency can't be realized without some amount of suffering. It is built into the healing process. This can help you take a different look at the meaning of your own suffering and its role in creating an authentic self. It should also be noted that the majority of this process is happening under the radar in your subconscious. Many mental health challenges are related to solving the problems in your subconscious mind that are ignored until they begin to influence your conscious mind.

As you become older and more sophisticated, your ability to perceive threats becomes more sophisticated too. The better you get at predicting possible outcomes the more you can imagine worst case scenarios that overwhelm you with anxiety and grief. Relationships can become more complicated making you doubt yourself in ways that can lead to shame and depression. Frustration over your lack of control can lead to anger.

All of the psychological dilemmas continue to work themselves out in your subconscious mind. Just like any other perceived threat they trigger your fears, affect your emotions, and compel you to figure out what they mean about your sense of well-being, and ultimately about who you are.

It runs in the background like a piece of software trying to solve the problem. Over and over again it reviews your experiences trying to reach a satisfactory conclusion. If you are unable to solve the puzzle it will continue endlessly, causing a feedback loop that can feel like a crisis. Without a clear sense of meaning it can eventually lead to self-doubt.

The loop is similar to the phenomenon known as an **ear worm**, a term for a song that gets stuck in your head that you find yourself repeating over and over again, usually out of your control. Scientists have learned that one way to get rid of an ear worm is to listen to the song from beginning to end and letting it finish to the very last note. [11] This, hopefully, will give your brain a sense that the song is over and the problem is solved. Like putting the last piece in a jigsaw puzzle, it feels complete.

The same thing happens when you are struggling either consciously or subconsciously with a psychological dilemma. The problem of what the experience means runs over and over again in your mind trying to solve the deeper problem about who you are. Many of my clients have agreed that it feels like they are looking for the missing pieces of a puzzle.

It should be noted that resiliency can't be realized without some amount of suffering. It is built into the healing process.

When you are plagued by one of these emotional feedback loops you may feel like you can't seem to find the missing pieces. What's more likely is that you have written some rules about who you are that don't match what you are experiencing. So the threat you feel can't seem to be resolved. You are living in a subconscious paradox that keeps trying to solve an impossible riddle.

In cases of trauma or abuse it can be especially debilitating. Having been a victim of a truly life threatening experience like a natural disaster or assault, or being subjected to prolonged abuse or neglect, a person can feel unable to resolve what this means about who they are. Their sense of self becomes intolerable because what happened to them is so unjustified and unacceptable.

This helps explain the symptoms of PTSD including flashbacks, recurring nightmares, racing thoughts, and extreme changes in personality. Sometimes victims of trauma aren't able to remember what happened to them, but they can suffer from distress for months and years after the threat occurred. In these cases the emotional immune system is working desperately in their subconscious to make sense of the senseless, trying to solve the puzzle about what it means for the person living through the tragedy.

Even when the puzzle is less extreme you can suffer a similar set of symptoms. Often unresolved grief from many years ago can lead to symptoms that interfere with daily living in the present. Anxiety, anger, shame, self-harm, and depression might also be part of your emotional immune system attempting to overcome a threat that seems so senseless it can't be resolved on its own.

It may be necessary for someone to take time out to process emotional pain in the same way they might need to heal from serious illness or physical injury.

In each of these cases your emotional immune system is using your body's natural processes to bring about healing. Just like physical illness, help may be needed to overcome the challenges you are facing. In the same way that physical therapy might help you recover from an injury, psychotherapy is useful in methodically solving the problems presented by the threats you have encountered. If your symptoms lead to thoughts and behaviors that make you unsafe to yourself or others you may need intervention and medication to ease emotional pain, prevent harm, and return to a healthy level of functioning.

Although it may seem perplexing, it's important to challenge the idea that all suffering is inherently wrong. You may have become convinced that disruptions in your emotional well-being are somehow a problem. Although they are certainly uncomfortable, the emotions you are having are not necessarily unhealthy.

Our culture has painted a picture of emotional healing as a blissful mountaintop experience overlooking a gorgeous sunset. In my experience nothing could be further from the truth. Healing is ugly. It is almost always unpleasant. Just like overcoming a virus or infection the illness is the cure. Building your emotional immune system not only includes suffering but requires it.[12]

Unfortunately some people magnify the problem by being upset with their own healing process. They feel anxious about being anxious. They get depressed about being depressed. They get angry about feeling angry. And to make matters worse they too quickly rely on medications and addictions to mask their symptoms before taking some time to trust and allow their natural emotional immune system to do its work.[13]

Medications can play a crucial role in easing suffering especially if someone is at risk of harming themselves. Anyone who has experienced the terrible pain of living with debilitating depression or anxiety can tell you that no one should have to suffer that much. But if medications are used carelessly without the support of competent person-centered therapy they could potentially interfere with the healing process.

The problem is that managing emotions in an authentic way can be terribly inconvenient in our world. As a culture we are not yet able to respect the emotional healing process as equivalent to the physical healing process. It may be necessary for someone to take time out to process emotional pain in the same way they might need to heal from serious illness or physical injury. Even people suffering severe psychological disorders should not ignore the value of relying on their emotional immune system to become more resilient.

I have many clients who tell me this idea has liberated them from a lifetime of feeling helpless to overcome their emotional challenges. Once they normalize the emotional immune process and make room for it to run its course they have found dramatic improvements in both their mental and physical health.

One client who had suffered sexual assault as a child came to me for depression and anxiety. She described a lifetime of shame and substance abuse trying to manage her emotions. Over time she became proficient at covering her pain with a well-manicured exterior, making sure she had it all together on the outside, but on the inside she felt like a fraud.

In treatment we took an inventory of the injustices she had faced. Her fear was that if she truly embraced her pain it would be too much to bear. I pointed out that as long as she was able to stay safe and free from self-harm her emotions had a purpose for her healing. I asked her to go home and allow the grief to happen and to trust her body and mind to heal itself.

For the next week she scheduled some time each day after work to cry and be alone with her emotions. Although her crying was briefly painful for a few minutes each day, she was surprised to find that it subsided within a relatively short amount of time.

Within a week she reported enormous progress and a new sense of freedom. She didn't feel so afraid of her grief. It wasn't lingering in the background like it did before. She had increased her ability to be confident without worrying as much about impressing others. Over a few weeks we worked together to reach a much greater sense of authenticity and purpose.

By finding the courage to trust your own emotional immune system you can begin to see yourself as capable and equipped to face your own fears about who you are. It can be a huge step toward understanding that you are already sufficient to be who you want to be.

Emotional Dashboard Lights

One of the more interesting exercises I have used in therapy as someone is telling a story about an emotional event is asking them to pause briefly and reflect on their physical symptoms in the present moment. They may be giving details about a time when they felt very angry, or scared, or especially sad as if they are reliving the experience. At that point I ask them where in their body do they feel that emotion. I may even ask them to point to it or act it out.

At first they are confused. Initially this seems like a strange idea. We are taught to believe that emotions happen only in the head. After a moment of reflection most of them can actually find it and point it out. Often they are surprised at this new way of thinking. Asking this question is useful in a couple of ways.

First it helps them recognize that thinking about an emotional experience that happened in the past can affect their present emotional state. Second, it can help them more readily recognize when the emotions are happening to them in the future. This is a type of mindfulness strategy that increases their emotional awareness and consequently their emotional intelligence.

The concept I'm describing is known as **interoception** or "internal awareness." A growing amount of research is being done to identify the many ways in which the human body makes sense of its own complex system of signals and sensations to create self-monitoring and perception.[14] This can lead to a much deeper and more useful understanding of healthy and unhealthy patterns of behavior.

When this level of awareness is disrupted it has been linked with a wide array of mental illnesses including eating disorders, mood disorders, spectrum disorders, and countless other physical ailments affecting the digestive and nervous systems. In contrast some progress has been made by practicing this awareness to increase resiliency in mental illness and alleviate many symptoms through meditation and body awareness training.[15]

By learning more about the connections between physical and emotional processes you can become more fully confident in accepting and appreciating your ability to manage the challenges you face.

By learning more about the connections between physical and emotional processes you can become more fully confident in accepting and appreciating your ability to manage the challenges you face. It can go a long way towards reducing what is basically an emotional allergic reaction.

When you suffer from allergies you are subject to your body's response to allergens in the environment. The initial reaction is useful to prevent certain substances from irritating parts of your body such as your lungs or your skin. Symptoms of swelling and fever are indicators that something is happening and you need to pay attention. When these symptoms go overboard, however, they can work against your body rather than to protect it.

In a similar way your emotional immune system has reactions that are inherently protective, but if they are ignored they can easily get out of hand and cause much more dangerous conditions. Just like a car has indicators to warn you of malfunctions, these **emotional dashboard lights** are mental signals telling you that the emotional immune system is doing something important underneath.

A person who recognizes these signals would be wise to pay attention and pull over to check on the engine. But that's not what many people do. Some people ignore them hoping they will go away. Others might even put a small piece of tape over them to cover them up. These might be temporary solutions, but it's likely that bigger problems will occur somewhere down the road.

In terms of resiliency this may represent an allergic reaction to a reasonably natural and healthy immune response. Many mental health issues may actually be an exaggerated response to what is a normal process of adapting to changes in the environment. If you are unwilling or unable to tolerate this level of discomfort you may interfere with this process by self-medicating with substances, or distract yourself with irrelevant or risky behaviors rather than trusting your own emotional immune system to overcome the challenge. As a result you find only temporary or insufficient relief and continue looking for solutions outside of yourself that further prevent your own healing.

Here is a list of some of the most common emotional dashboard lights you are likely to see as allergic reactions to your emotional immune system. Remember that although these symptoms may be uncomfortable, they are really a signal that something deeper is going on. While they do represent legitimate issues that need to be addressed, focusing only on these symptoms will distract you from dealing with the important issues lying underneath.

Anger – A great deal of attention is often placed on feelings of anger, and that's the whole point. Anger is supposed to cover up feelings that are hard to live with. It may be loud and destructive, or it may be hidden and seething. It may be about injustice over wrongs that have been done. Or it may be about something that was lost or taken away. Regardless, it is linked to an underlying frustration about being out of control.

Whenever this feeling pops up it is helpful to ask what is behind the door of anger. What is your anger being used to conceal? Very likely it is trying to protect you from a feeling of vulnerability that you haven't yet learned to accept. By learning to use anger in a healthy way to focus on what you can control, you will be more effective at moving towards a meaningful and authentic life.

Anxiety – Concern about the future is perfectly normal and helpful to a large extent. But when anxiety becomes irrational it triggers a survival instinct that clouds your judgement. If you ignore anxiety or allow it to become pervasive it can lead to real physical symptoms and severe difficulties in functioning.

It can be helpful to recognize that the only reason you become afraid is because you care about something. Your fears exist because of your values, not in spite of them. Conventional wisdom tells us that we should talk ourselves out of being afraid. But by looking directly at your fears and identifying the values they represent you can learn a lot about who you are and define strategies to act on your values instead of living in crippling fear.

Blame – Any effort to assign blame is usually misguided and unproductive. At its essence is the attempt to make someone or something other than yourself responsible for the emotions that are being felt. While another person's actions may be the cause of your problem, they can never be the cause of your emotions.

As soon as you find yourself looking for someone to blame choose instead to identify your own feelings and take responsibility for them. Learn to recognize the ways in which you expect other people to change so that you can feel better, and then find ways to change the situation yourself. Choose to be authentic in your response so that your efforts help you live with integrity and confidence.

Depression – The depths of despair can be a terrible place to live. If you have suffered depression you probably know how helpless it can make you feel. When it seems too difficult or impossible to change your situation it will likely lead to an even greater sense of hopelessness.

But the symptoms of depression are the result of a vital step in the process of personal growth. What depression is telling you is that WHO you are on the inside doesn't match HOW you are on the outside. This means that depression is not just a crisis of living, but also a crisis of self. By working towards authenticity you can become more capable of seeing depression as a guide towards the areas of your self-image that need to be nurtured or empowered.

Shame – Nothing short circuits your emotional immune system more than feelings of shame. How can you possibly learn to heal your sense of self when you have already decided that you are unworthy of compassion and forgiveness? Shame feels like a trap you can never escape. The truth is that shame is a trap you have set for yourself, and that means you are the only one who can set yourself free.

When shame shows up it is good time to listen to your inner dialogue and start asking where those messages are coming from. Sometimes shame comes from voices outside of you that want you to feel inadequate so they can take advantage of you. Sometimes shame comes from within as a way to excuse your lack of courage. And sometimes shame is merely a symptom of emotional fatigue. No matter where it comes from, shame is an invitation to accept and maybe even celebrate your own limitations as you embrace your move in the direction of authenticity.

Streamlining Your Values

What I'm suggesting by all of this is that your search for authenticity must include an ever increasing tolerance for the discomfort associated with building resiliency. Your emotional immune system is the first line of defense in withstanding the storms that come your way. Your ability to trust this essential process has a direct impact on how well you develop an authentic sense of self and the values you invest in on a daily basis.

I often encourage people to become comfortable with their discomfort. The challenge is learning how to interpret those storms more accurately in order to increase confidence and take advantage of our built-in system of resiliency.

Most people are surprised to find out that the process of learning is really more about forgetting than remembering. Much of what your brain does happens under the radar. It controls your nervous system, hormones, digestion and other subconscious involuntary processes that are needed to keep going, and keep growing. The conscious part—all the stuff you think and feel and perceive—is really only a small part of the overall job description of your brain. And even that is limited by what your brain makes a point to filter out.

At any one moment there is an entire spectrum of stimuli that are being experienced by your brain that it has learned to ignore in order for you to focus on the stream of consciousness you call your thoughts. The feeling of your clothes against your skin, the sound of your own heartbeat, even the nose on your face are all part of the world that your brain intentionally removes from your thoughts so you can get something done. In reality your brain spends more time forgetting and filtering things out than it does collecting things to remember.

If you were to look at your brain in a microscope you would see trillions of connections between neurons that act as pathways to trillions of other neurons and nerve endings throughout your body. In order to learn you are constantly keeping track of the connections that lead to a rewarding experience like a hug, or a taste of ice cream, or a solution to a problem.

The positive result leads to a surge of dopamine in your brain that reinforces the connection and it becomes stronger. Other connections that aren't being used begin to fade and literally wither like a dried up twig. This process happens with lightning speed every second of every day rewiring your brain in response to your experiences. [16]

When you are solving the problem of self every tiny conclusion you reach about who you are gets reinforced in exactly this way. It's not a stretch to say that your entire identity is actually a collection of neurons in your brain. And because you are a living breathing human being, these neurons are constantly being challenged by changes in the environment.

Every experience you process through your emotional immune system is contributing to the overall assessment of your values and defining who you think you are. When your values collide they are not just creating an identity crisis, they are guiding you towards a more efficient and authentic sense of self. The discomfort associated with this ongoing process is more than just beneficial. It's an vital part of your survival and well-being.

> *Authentic people allow crisis to teach them more about who they are, and more importantly who they aren't.*

This doesn't mean we should minimize the pain that people feel. But it must be a part of how we interpret and respond to mental illness. When people find themselves suffering from anxiety, depression, and grief we can choose to avoid the stigma and begin looking for the strengths that will result in greater resiliency.

Authentic people do this all the time. They recognize the value of their own suffering. They give themselves permission to experience it without judging themselves or others who may have caused it. They allow crisis to teach them more about who they are, and more importantly who they aren't.

If you've ever spent time with old people you may have some idea what this looks like. By the time you reach a ripe old age you will have learned a thing or two about what does and doesn't matter. You might call it wisdom, but it's really just the end result of a lifetime spent forgetting things that just don't really matter.

There's no reason to wait until you are old to become authentic. Take advantage of the hard work you are already doing. Tomorrow is yet another opportunity to face a few more storms and learn a few more things about yourself.

If you learn to see the value of your discomfort, you can get much better at streamlining your values and focusing on being the person you really want to be.

CHAPTER 3 NOTES

[8] Felitti, V. J., Anda, R. F., Nordenberg, D., Williamson, D. F., Spitz, A. M., Edwards, V., Koss, M. P., ... Marks, J. S. (June 01, 2019). Relationship of Childhood Abuse and Household Dysfunction to Many of the Leading Causes of Death in Adults: The Adverse Childhood Experiences (ACE) Study. *American Journal of Preventive Medicine, 56*, 6, 774-786.

[9] Koubeissi, M. Z., Bartolomei, F., Bartolomei, F., Bartolomei, F., Beltagy, A., & Picard, F. (January 01, 2014). Electrical stimulation of a small brain area reversibly disrupts consciousness. Epilepsy and Behavior, 37, 32-35.

[10] Crick, F., & Koch, C. (January 01, 2003). A framework for consciousness. *Nature Neuroscience, 6*, 2, 119-26.

[11] Victoria, J. W., Lassi, A. L., Kelly, J., & Lauren, S. (January 31, 2014). Sticky Tunes: How Do People React to Involuntary Musical Imagery?. *Plos One, 9*, 1.)

[12] Brinkmann, S. (January 02, 2017). Perspectives on diagnosed suffering. *Nordic Psychology, 69*, 1, 1-4.

[13] Ford, B. Q., Lam, P., John, O. P., & Mauss, I. B. (January 01, 2018). The Psychological Health Benefits of Accepting Negative Emotions and Thoughts: Laboratory, Diary, and Longitudinal Evidence. *Journal of Personality and Social Psychology, 115*, 6, 1075-1092.

[14] Shah, P., Catmur, C., & Bird, G. (August 01, 2017). From heart to mind: Linking interoception, emotion, and theory of mind. *Cortex, 93*, 220-223.

[15] Plans, D. (2019, February 05). We've Lost Touch with Our Bodies. Retrieved from https://blogs.scientificamerican.com/observations/weve-lost-touch-with-our-bodies/

[16] Infobase & National Geographic Society (U.S.). (2015). *Science of Babies.*

Summary

- Resiliency is a person's ability to withstand and even thrive in the face of difficult circumstances.

- The emotional immune system works to strengthen resiliency by recognizing and learning from threats in the environment.

- By increasing internal awareness of emotions a person can significantly improve their mental health.

- Learning to appreciate the discomfort of emotional healing is essential to clarifying values and establishing an authentic sense of self.

Reflections

1. How do you respond differently when you experience physical illness compared to your emotional difficulties?

2. What is an emotional concern that used to bother you that no longer feels like a threat?

3. Describe a time when you recognized an emotional dashboard light. How well did you respond and what would you do differently?

4. Name a celebrity or a person in your life who you would consider a healthy role model for resiliency and authenticity.

5. What are some values that used to be important to you but no longer seem to matter?

4 - AUTHENTIC INTENTIONS
FACING DISILLUSIONMENT

Nearly everyone has an opinion about magicians. The point of magic is to cause some level of confusion by creating the illusion that something is real, even when you know it isn't. Some people thoroughly enjoy watching them perform routines that leave them confounded. Others are not so impressed, watching with a skeptical eye trying to figure out how the trick is done.

If you ask people their preference you will usually end up with two separate categories of onlookers. There are those who want to know how the trick is done and those who don't. This is likely true for one reason. Once you know how the trick is done you can never not know. No matter how hard you try, the illusion is gone and you can never enjoy the trick the same way again.

Magic can be entertaining because it reminds you of all the times in your life when you thought you knew how life is supposed to work and then it turns out differently than expected. This loss of innocence can be fun when it's just a performance. But when it happens in your real life it can be anything but funny.

When people come into therapy they have usually lost some sense of certainty about life. They thought they had a grasp on reality, but something has happened that made them doubt themselves, or the people they know, or even the universe itself. Unlike a magic trick this feeling is terribly unsettling.

One person might tell a story about working their whole lives to build a career that makes them a lot of money or prestige, only to find out that it never lives up to the life they imagined. They keep striving for more hoping it will one day feel satisfying. At the end of it all they find they have sacrificed so much for a dream that never came true.

Another person might long for a relationship that fulfills them and makes them whole. They fall in love over and over again thinking that each lover is the one they were meant to be with for a lifetime of romance and happiness. But over time their hopes are dashed and they are left feeling wounded and unworthy.

In each case they are facing some level of disillusionment. It feels like the worst possible thing that could happen. When I hear these stories I like to point out that the opposite is true. People who are living in this new reality have literally become **dis-<u>illusioned</u>** and can no longer be blinded by their own false assumptions.

The word **illusion** comes from the Latin word **ludere** which means "a play or a performance." It calls to mind a stage with actors performing their lines as the story unfolds. We each play our parts in the drama convinced that the whole thing is real. But when we see behind the scenes and the masks are removed we find out it was all just make believe.[17]

Coming to terms with disillusionment is a vital part of finding your authenticity. The daily drama you live with is a direct result of your ideas about what matters and how you see yourself in your own story. Your choices are deeply influenced by the assumptions you make about your ability to create the life that matches your identity.

When those assumptions turn out to be false the illusion is ruined and you might lose faith in yourself. You can become anxious or depressed, worried that you are failing in some way. Or you could become angry at people and situations that won't conform to your reality. All of this leads to a crisis that must be resolved in order to feel safe again.

The secret to facing disillusionment is discovering that you are part of a huge magic trick. In the same way that a magician is pretending to pull a rabbit out of his hat, you live your life under an illusion that you are in control of events and relationships around you. That's why you might become so upset when the truth is revealed and you face the fact that you have very little control over the things that happen to you.

In order to live an authentic life you must learn to recognize when you are falling for the illusion, and then accept that you are part of a huge game that we are all playing. Like children playing make-believe we are all acting out a daily drama, wearing a mask to hide our true identity, and pretending to be in charge of the story.

How The Trick Is Done

Most people come to me with varying degrees of disillusionment. They have become frustrated about their life and have no idea what to do. Very often they have been trying to make something happen in their life and have reached a point of despair, with no more motivation or energy to continue. That's when I tell them, as compassionately as possible, that it's probably a good thing they have given up.

In order to illustrate this point I draw a large triangle and at the top I write the word **DISILLUSIONMENT**. Then I point to the top of the triangle and say, "This is where you are right now." I then explain that although they feel like they have reached the bottom, they have actually reached the top of an important peak. And from the top of that peak they are able to see more clearly than ever before. They have reached a valuable turning point that may be rather painful, but that is because they have just been through a tremendous ordeal.

This is what it sounds like when I take them through the following steps:

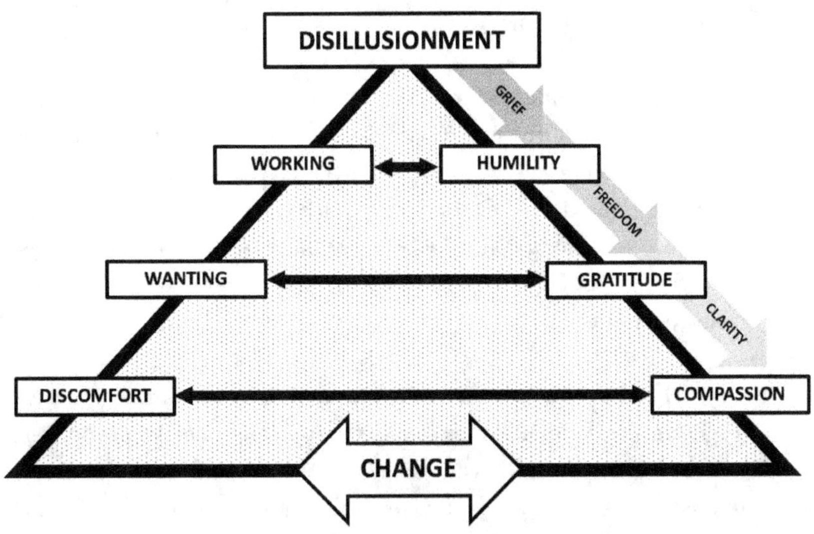

1. Discomfort – At the source of all discomfort is the reality of change. When the weather changes you become uncomfortable and adjust to the new temperature. When you get hungry your stomach growls and you start looking for food. When you fall in love it can become unbearable to live apart. All of these changes cause different types of discomfort. So discomfort is not really a good or bad thing. It's merely a fact of life.

2. Wanting – In the simplest terms, discomfort and motivation are the same thing. Everything you want is an attempt to satisfy your perceived needs as they arise. As a human you have a relentless drive to invent countless strategies to fulfill your needs. Wanting is a driving force for much of the pain you feel as you live with a sense of deficiency, worried that you are missing out, focused on all the things you don't have, or believe you should have.

3. Working – Convinced that you are missing something in life you will find yourself striving to achieve your goals to fulfill your needs. It feels like you are pushing a boulder up a hill, and it gets harder and harder the higher you get. You might be able to convince yourself not to give up. You are certain that if you just try a little harder you can find happiness and fulfillment. But at some point you will become exhausted, unable to push any further. As soon as you let go, the boulder rolls back to the bottom. Then you have to decide if you are going back down the hill to try it all over again.

4. Disillusionment – From the top you look down at the boulder that you have been pushing up a hill for so long, facing the realization that you just can't do it anymore. You may have been successful before. But this one boulder seems to be too much for you. Despite your best efforts you are no longer able to deny that there are some things you just can't achieve. And this is when you lose your greatest illusion… the illusion of control.

5. Humility – In this illustration the definition of humility is a clear recognition of your own limitations. On the other side of the hill you were convinced that you could overcome whatever challenge you were facing. But on this side of the hill you have no choice but to accept that you are unable to change the situation. In the beginning this leads to an enormous amount of grief. You may experience anger, depression, bargaining, denial and all of the other symptoms that come from losing something you never really had. But once you reach acceptance and surrender to the truth of your humility you will begin to experience a refreshing sense of freedom.

6. Gratitude – As you embrace this freedom you will feel a new sense of abundance. Once you let go of your illusion of control you can begin to live more authentically, unhindered by all the wasted energy trying to achieve unreachable goals. It will be much easier to recognize and appreciate how much you already have because you have begun to recognize how little you actually need.

7. Compassion – The final stage of this journey ends with a twist. Although it started with discomfort, it was never leading away from it but back towards discomfort instead. Because change is constant, so is discomfort. The goal is not to eliminate discomfort but to live with it. The word **passion** means "suffering" as in something we love so much it hurts. So the word **compassion** literally means "suffering with." At this stage you can practice a level of engagement with yourself and others that doesn't depend on control but simply accepting discomfort as part of the healing process.

There are few things to remember as you look at this journey from a practical perspective. First, you must recognize that it is built on the concept of opposites. Discomfort is the opposite of compassion. Gratitude is the opposite of wanting. Humility is the opposite of work. In each case the loss of your illusion of control liberates you from the burden of striving and suffering in a way that leads to frustration and fear.

Once you learn to live with compassion you are no longer driven by so much anxiety. You don't have to assume that your discomfort is somehow your fault because you can't control the universe. Once you learn to live with gratitude and humility your workload will decrease significantly because your **"wantload"** has decreased as well.

Second, you must come to terms with the idea that acceptance of your limitations is not a sign of weakness. In order to live a genuinely authentic life it may require an unprecedented amount of courage. It can't be overstated how important it is to process the grief that comes from letting go of something you've given so much of yourself to achieve. That grief is necessary to fully accept that you have been living a lie.

It is possible that you will experience a certain degree of shame because you think you aren't good enough to make some fantasy come true. It might be a career goal, or a marriage, or some other aspect of your life that you have decided has to be controlled in some way in order for you to be happy. Whenever you are thinking about letting go of something ask yourself "Am I quitting, or am I setting myself free?"

Third, when you have an accurate understanding of your limitations you also have a clear view of your values. This is essential to living an authentic life. All of your energy can be used more efficiently because you no longer have to burden yourself with meaningless pursuits. Instead you will find your life more fulfilling and satisfying that you ever thought possible. And the irony is that such abundance and meaning have been there all along.

Finally, once you are aware that you are living an abundant authentic life, you will start to see where other people are on the journey. You will see them pushing their own boulders up their own hills and remember how it felt for you. Just as you needed to come to your own crisis in order to see yourself more clearly, you will learn that you can't convince anyone to open their eyes until they have worn themselves out.

That's how the trick is done. And once you know how it works you can't go back.

Living With Discomfort

There is a classic study about the relative happiness of lottery winners when compared to quadriplegic accident victims.[18] In the study they asked each group a year after their major life events had occurred to rate their degree of happiness when participating in ordinary activities like eating breakfast or talking with a friend. Researchers were surprised to find that there was no significant difference in the amount of pleasure they each found in everyday life.

That doesn't mean that paraplegics are just as happy as lottery winners. But it does point out that happiness is not inherently linked to your circumstances or in the activities you do every day. It would be tempting to conclude that happiness is all a state of mind. But I don't really think that's the lesson either.

What I think it means is that happiness is beside the point. The idea that you can seek and find a state of bliss or comfort is just another boulder that you can push up a hill. It is an illusion that you want to believe in very much like a magic trick. Over time you will catch a hint or two that it might not be possible. That thought can be very disturbing if you are truly attached to it.

Depending on the severity of the situation once the reality sets in it can lead to a great deal of despair. Many people are unable to cope with this and suffer tremendously at the thought that they can never really control how happy they are. So our culture has fabricated a multitude of ways to medicate or distract us from this basic truth about our existence.

Your response to the uncertainty of life is a really good place to start in coming to terms with your authentic self. It is the recipe of your personality. Remember that your brain is biologically driven to solve the problem of self by recognizing and overcoming perceived threats. So in order to discover your authentic self you need to be fully and completely honest about the world you live in.

> *There is a direct correlation between your ability to fully accept your own limitations and your ability to live with authenticity.*

Your disillusionment is a gift. It is the only way to strip down all of the magic tricks you have been falling for that have you convinced of your invulnerability. As long as you falsely believe you can control the feelings and actions of other people enough to make you happy you will be perpetually frustrated. As long as you deny your vulnerability in an uncertain world you will be haunted by self-doubt. There is a direct correlation between your ability to fully accept your own limitations and your ability to live with authenticity.

You must trust your own emotional immune system to help you cope with this reality. There is no short cut to emotional health when it comes to facing the grief you may experience as you lose your illusions of control. This is quite possibly the hardest work you will do in working towards an authentic life. But it is necessary to gain the resiliency to navigate the unfamiliar world you will be living in.[19]

There is no going back. Once you know how the trick is done you can't put it back the way it was. Even so, the way forward can be incomparably rewarding, because what will happen next is more fulfilling than any boulder you've tried to conquer.

Many people tell me that on the other side of their grief is a profound sense of clarity. Once you accept your limitations and eliminate your anxiety about manipulating, or changing, or fixing things beyond your control, you can become more certain about what you genuinely care about, and how to live authentically. In the midst of your crisis you may feel afraid of being helpless, but once the pressure to control others is lifted you will feel empowered to do things that really matter to you.

The fear of missing out is replaced with a streamlined set of values because you are able to recognize the abundance you already possess.[20] Ironically this is not always connected to your access to wealth, opportunities, privilege, or other resources. People all along the economic spectrum struggle with feeling cheated out of what they deserve. But that idea itself is an illusion.

Your journey through disillusionment and despair into freedom and abundance is the foundation of finding your purpose and meaning.

Who deserves to be wealthy or poor? Who decides how justice should be determined? How do we choose what to accept or reject about the hand we have been dealt? What is fair and unfair in the world? All of these questions are valid and important, but none of them can be answered outside of the narrative about who you are.

Until you reach a place of clarity about your authentic values you will be dissatisfied by your efforts to seek justice or fairness, no matter how valiant or heroic. By the same token, you must first resolve your own insecurities before you can appreciate the struggles you witness in the lives of those around you. There is no compassion without gratitude, and there is no gratitude without humility. These are irreplaceable ingredients in the recipe of authenticity.

Remember compassion is not the opposite of suffering but the ability to live with it. Your journey through disillusionment and despair into freedom and abundance is the foundation of finding your purpose and meaning. By removing the distractions and illusions about your ability to control people and events, you can focus on the priorities that bring you genuine fulfillment.

Once you accept and appreciate the role of discomfort you can begin to use it for your own advantage. As you encounter challenges big and small you can decide how they will contribute to your sense of self. If you are able to see discomfort as normal, then living with it becomes a choice rather than an obligation. By practicing gratitude you can begin to reframe more experiences not just as things you have to do, but things you get to do.

Do you HAVE to take the kids to school or do you GET to take them to school. Do you HAVE to go to work or do you GET to go to work. Do you HAVE to pay taxes or do you GET to pay taxes. In each case the action is the same but your mindset creates the possibility that the activity is not just happening TO you but FOR you in order to live out your values.

Even if it feels idealistic, that doesn't make it wrong. Any change like this will be unfamiliar and uncomfortable because it requires you to question your values and identity. As long as you see yourself as a passive victim of circumstances you don't have to accept responsibility for the outcome of your choices. Once you learn how to live in humility and abundance you can stop living with a mindset of deficiency.

Choosing Your Own Discomfort

Since one of the primary functions of your brain is to solve problems, many of your problems may simply be the result of your brain looking for problems to solve. Consciously and subconsciously your brain is actively engaged in managing discomfort as it arises from second to second. From the most basic needs of air, food, and shelter to the more aspirational goals of learning, being creative, and making the world a better place, your brain is solving problems and consolidating your internal concept of who you are.

At a basic level you are always seeking a balance between two ends of a see-saw in order to feel some sense of control over the changes that

happen all the time. As I've been pointing out, this feeling of control is very often an illusion. The more you learn about yourself the better you are at finding a healthy balance.

The see-saw is always in balance between two opposing forms of anxiety. At one end is the anxiety you get when you feel like you have very little or no control over what is happening to you. This anxiety is called **frustration**. Whenever someone starts talking about frustration what I hear is that they want to control something and it isn't working out. By identifying what you can and cannot control you can more easily find an action plan to help reduce your anxiety.

On the other end of the see-saw is an anxiety you feel when you have too much control of your life. This anxiety is called **boredom**. You might not think of boredom as a type of anxiety but it can actually be more intense. What boredom means is that in some area of your life all of your needs have been met, and you are looking for a new problem to solve. This is the mechanism that drives motivation towards growth and self-improvement.

It's a foundation of motivational psychology that needs must be met in a certain order.[21] At the foundation are your physiological needs like food and shelter. Above that are your psychological needs including social and intellectual interests. At the top are your fulfillment needs for, meaning and self-actualization (which is literally the point of this book.) In order for you to actualize your "self" all of your other needs must be met.

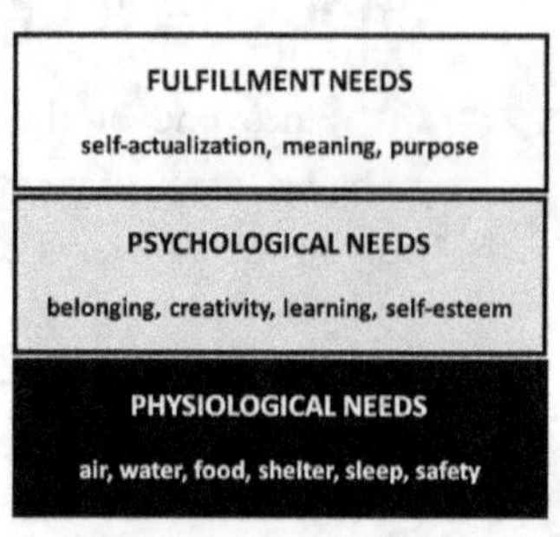

So if you are starving or feel unsafe you will be unable to focus on learning or being a functional part of society. You must have your primary concerns met before moving on to more sophisticated pursuits. What it also means is that once you have – or believe you have – met all of your needs you are driven to go looking for the next set of needs on your list.

What this looks like in the real world is living your life in search of new problems to solve. If you are in an actual crisis like a natural disaster or life threatening emergency you will instinctively begin working on the most basic needs to survive and abandon less important ones until you are ready to move on. If there is no emergency it is very normal to invent problems and respond to them with a similar amount of urgency.

Think of children who find themselves with nothing to do. It won't take long before they begin to complain about being bored. What this actually means is that all of their needs have been met and they have become too comfortable. They will begin to look for ways to become uncomfortable – on purpose. They might pick on their sister, or go for a walk, or play a game.

Once each of those things get boring they will find ways to make them more challenging. How much does it take to make her angry? How high can I climb this tree? How can I change the rules to make this game more interesting?

It's not that different for adults. How much money can I make? How high can I climb the corporate ladder? How can I change the rules to make my life more interesting?

Boredom is the fuel for change. It's just as important as frustration in motivating you to take action. It influences you daily and shapes the strategies you invent to grow towards the ultimate goal of self-actualization; becoming who you think you ought to be.

The problem is that most people are not in charge of how this process works. A lot of times when clients come into counseling they have been on auto-pilot for most of their lives. They have assumed their relationships, their careers, and their health will just run themselves. Sometimes it has worked for a long time until they reach a fork in the road, or the wheels falls off, or they run out of fuel. Any of these challenges can make them unsure of about who they are so they no longer know what to do about it.

If you want to get back on track you have to be intentional about how you live. You have to pay attention to what's happening on the inside as well as on the outside to make sure your needs are getting met the way YOU want them to be. Otherwise it will just happen TO you and not FOR you. You must choose your own discomfort, or it will be chosen for you.

Authentic people choose their values before they choose their goals. They learn how to stop being defined by their circumstances and work towards living with integrity and resiliency in every situation. They see the purpose of their discomfort as an opportunity to become more in tune with their authentic self and let go of any illusions that distract them.

CHAPTER 4 NOTES

[17] Watts, A. (2000). The philosophies of Asia: Essential lectures of Alan Watts. California: Electronic University.

[18] Brickman, P., Coates, D., & Janoff-Bulman, R. (January 01, 1978). Lottery winners and accident victims: is happiness relative?. Journal of Personality and Social Psychology, 36, 8, 917-27.

[19] Shallcross, A. J., Troy, A. S., Boland, M., & Mauss, I. B. (September 01, 2010). Let it be: Accepting negative emotional experiences predicts decreased negative affect and depressive symptoms. *Behaviour Research and Therapy, 48, 9, 921-929.*

[20] Brinkmann, S. (2019). The joy of missing out: The art of self-restraint in an age of excess.

[21] Maslow, A. H. (January 01, 1943). A theory of human motivation. Psychological Review, 50, 4, 370-396.

Summary

- The crisis of disillusionment is an essential part of becoming more authentic.

- Accepting your limitations may be a painful process but it eventually leads to a newfound sense of clarity and freedom.

- Learning to live with discomfort can be a foundation for building a more meaningful and compassionate life.

- How you decide to respond to frustration and boredom can determine how successful you are at meeting your own needs for personal fulfillment.

Reflections

1. How do you manage your feelings when you find out something you believed in strongly turns out to be disappointing or untrue?

2. What is something you are having a hard time admitting that you can't control?

3. What are some things that you feel you deserve or don't deserve that cause emotional distress?

4. Describe a time when you created a challenge for yourself because you were bored.

5. What part of your life is on auto-pilot? Name some ways you can be more intentional about making improvements.

5 - AUTHENTIC RELATIONSHIPS
LOOKING IN THE MIRROR

When most people think about psychology they almost always imagine Sigmund Freud sitting in a chair listening to a person on a couch talking about their deepest, darkest secrets. He started using "talking therapy" in 1886 to demonstrate that discussing your inner demons could make a difference in your mental health.

Before that people suffering from mental illness were either drugged or received medical treatments that today would be considered torture. If that didn't work they were typically locked away in a hospital or someone's attic. Freud's contribution made it possible for mental health to be administered in a more humane and rational way.

Perhaps the most famous protégé of Sigmund Freud was Carl Jung. With the development of **analytical psychology** Jung used therapy to identify the components of a person's internal psyche and how they played a critical role in the formation of their personality. In this way he was able to address their unconscious insecurities, anxieties, and internal conflicts that expressed themselves consciously through psychological processes.

In summarizing a central idea about the impact of relationships on our sense of self Carl Jung provided this essential truth. [22]

**Everything that irritates us about others
can lead us to an understanding of ourselves.**

It is impossible to summarize Jung's ideas with a single quote. But for our purposes we can use this as a launchpad for a practical discussion about how to use relationships to live a more authentic life.

Why Some People Bother You

Authenticity cannot be gained outside the context of relationships. In fact it's not possible to even have an identity without recognizing that others exist. That's how you come to the conclusion that you are you, and others are not you.

As an infant this is one of the most important ideas you encounter—me and not me. Somewhere in the first few months of life, after your physical birth, you experience the birth of your ego. You don't know it's happening, but without it you could not develop as a human being. By the time you become a toddler you are not only aware of your own ego, but you become quite adamant that you have your own preferences and abilities. This results in a steady stream of temper tantrums and unusual wardrobe choices.

At the same time you are developing attachment patterns that will shape the way you relate to others for the rest of your life including social skills, work relationships, family dynamics, and future life partners. This universal milestone is a momentous step in the growth of every human learning how to be a self.

It doesn't have to be a big deal that you came from any particular family or what experiences you may have lived through as a child. As we've said before humans are equipped with a built in emotional immune system to cope and adapt to the challenges that they face along the way. A key component of your emotional immune system is the instinctive ability to use your relationships with others to come to a deeper understanding of your values.

What Carl Jung could not have known when he developed his theory is that a century later scientists would discover a type of brain cell called **mirror neurons** that allow people to actually feel what someone else is doing. When you watch someone doing something, some of the neurons in your brain are activated as if you are doing it too. [23]

If you see someone hitting a baseball your mirror neurons cause you to think you are also hitting a baseball. If you watch someone eating a piece of pizza there are some of your brain cells also eating a pizza. If you notice someone crying there is a part of you that also feels sad. This is likely why laughter and yawning are contagious, and it's the foundation for empathy and our ability to learn skills from watching others.

It helps explain why we are attracted to some people, and why other people really bother us. With the presence of mirror neurons in our brain it is next to impossible to interact with other people and not have some sort of reaction to them. With all of this going on in our subconscious we are programmed to have a reaction to people whether we like it or not.

This also lines up with the concept of **complementary immune systems**. Researchers have found that people may be attracted to others with genetic codes that provide immune systems that are different than their own, a process guided subconsciously by their sense of smell.[24] The idea is that immune systems which are too similar don't provide enough diversity to help our species survive.

If we combine the concept of mirror neurons to the theory of our emotional immune system it gives an important insight into what relationships are all about. From an psychological standpoint you are attracted to people who can give you something you can't do for yourself. This does not automatically mean that, as the old saying goes, opposites attract. But it does mean that the people you are drawn to intellectually, romantically, sexually or socially, are people who you subconsciously believe will help you fill in your perceived blanks.

Every relationship is reflecting back to you a world of useful information that you may or may not be able to see about yourself.

As you strive for authenticity this insight can help you understand what is going on when you meet people who make you feel strongly in some way. Something about their personality is either consciously or subconsciously teaching you about yourself. Every relationship can serve as a **psychological mirror** to help you solve the problem of self.

Sometimes when you look into the psychological mirror you see things you like. Maybe that person you find so intriguing is reminding you about something you want to see in yourself. Or they may be validating a certain aspect of your character that you hope other people will admire.

Other times you may look in the psychological mirror and see things you don't like. You meet people who make you feel uncomfortable or even downright angry. It's possible they are reflecting something back to you that you don't want to see in yourself. Or they may be reminding you about a habit or a trait that you personally find intolerable. They are reminding you about something you would never want anyone to think about you.

This concept can be life changing when you start to see the world as place that is full of mirrors. Every relationship is reflecting back to you a world of useful information that you may or may not be able to see about yourself. From your most intimate family and friends, to the strangers you pass on the street, you are constantly working on developing a sense of who you are as you compare and contrast yourself to all of the people around you.

What is it about that coworker who bothers you so much? What does she do that makes you uncomfortable? Maybe her behavior triggers an insecurity you still need to resolve in yourself. Maybe she acts in a way that reminds you of who you used to be, and you subconsciously worry it might still be true.

What about your ex-husband who still treats you unjustly? His verbal abuse continues to haunt you even as you try to schedule his visits with the kids. It may take years to become resilient enough to face him without fear. When you see him as a mirror you can be reminded that you are not him, and he has no right to define you. Over time you can learn what he has taught you about becoming the person you want to be.

This is common among members of families who are simultaneously closely bonded and striving for individuality. You can't help but see the similarities that remind you of yourself both physically and emotionally. From their mannerisms and habits, to their belief system and traditions, there are lots of opportunities to reflect things back to you that can be either validating or utterly repulsive.

A great deal of politics and culture is driven by this impulse to react emotionally to images depicted in the media. The convenience of portraying people as good guys and bad guys allows you to be swayed by your own insecurities. And it makes for a powerful marketing strategy to tap into your subconscious desires for belonging and acceptance.

It isn't necessary to see these instincts with cynicism, or as a sign of weakness, but rather as a valuable tool to gain insight into your own internal processes that are already happening because they need to be happening. The people who bother you, as well as the people you like, are all components of a natural mechanism that can successfully inoculate you to their influence. Just like a virus that we overcome they can strengthen your authenticity, but only if you encounter them with confidence.

The Problem With People

A while ago I picked up on a trend with my clients that highlighted the importance of relationships. Within a single week I had three separate clients of different ages and backgrounds tell me that they felt lost – and they used that word specifically. They each told me that they were increasingly unsure about who they are. Over the next month or so I began to hear it all around me among clients, friends, and in the media. Once I started looking it became far too common to ignore, so I became curious.

As I examined the possible causes I discovered research about the impact of social media on a person's self-image. A primary facet of social media is that it is heavily curated by both the users and the platform itself [25]. Extensive work has gone into creating software with elaborate algorithms that allow users to exclude ideas, images, and entire groups of people that they don't like. By design social media, and media in general, intentionally omit content which runs contrary to the user's preferred point of view.

For every perfect picture there are hundreds that get deleted. Headlines and articles are written to maximize emotional reactions rather than to inform or educate. Scientific journals are published for the sole purpose of legitimizing biased results. Entire media networks conspire to distribute ideas that are blatantly one-sided. As a result we are overwhelmed with a world that is full of circus mirrors that give us false reflections of ourselves. We can't make sense of who we are because the mirrors we are using are lying to us.

Unless you are exposed to challenging situations you will be surrounded by people, images, and ideas that only validate the mask you hide behind. Even though this sounds appealing and comfortable, doing so will shield you from aspects in your subconscious that need to be addressed. The longer you hide from yourself by avoiding people who bother you, the more painful it will be when you begin to face your own truth.

The benefits of living with people you don't like far outweigh the costs of isolation.[26] Genuine authenticity requires you to become increasingly more comfortable with people who reflect all of your personality, not just the good stuff. The long term goal is to become resilient enough to interact with unpleasant people without blaming them for your insecurities.

However, this poses a bigger problem. How do you learn to live with, and even benefit from, your relationship with ALL people when some of them can be verifiably threatening? Of course there are the curmudgeons and cranks that get on your nerves. But there are also criminals and predators who are actually looking for a chance to hurt you. Learning about yourself from someone who bothers you does not also mean you should be victimized by their behavior.

Certainly there is a need to set clear boundaries to protect yourself. But in order to become resilient you will need to manage your feelings of fear to process your emotions and find meaning in the experience. This is the pathway to authenticity, through your emotional immune system. Without this process you can find yourself trapped in a subconscious loop of unresolved insecurities. Your brain wants to solve the problem of people. So you would be better off finding a strategy to meet this need instead of just ignoring it or feeling sorry for yourself.

> *Genuine authenticity requires you to become increasingly more comfortable with people who reflect all of your personality, not just the good stuff.*

The good news is… I have a plan. As you might expect it has a little to do with the nature of authenticity itself. I have come to believe that authenticity is the only reasonable answer to the larger problem of living with other people.

As I began my work on authenticity I began to ask myself if encouraging people to be their true self was actually ethical. Obviously I want certain people to be authentic—especially people just like me who I find interesting and pleasant to be around.

But what about the people I don't like? Why would I encourage them to be more authentic? That could make them even more unlikable, at least to me. How can I justify promoting authenticity when it could potentially backfire and lead to a whole bunch of unpleasant people becoming more and more authentically unpleasant?

Do I even have the right to make this decision? Who am I to determine who should be authentic and who shouldn't? How can I decide this with any sense of integrity? All of these questions are wrapped up in my own authenticity about being true to my values. They forced me to take a hard look at how good decisions get made.

There is a lot of information in the world about ethics and ethical behavior. If you want to study the field of ethics you will quickly learn that every field of study and professional occupation has their own take on the basic principles of ethical decision making. As someone who strives for practicality I decided to boil it down to the most basic explanation I could manage. By doing so I was able to provide a framework for my clients to help them use ethics in their daily life and to apply it in the context of relationships.

As it turns out the idea of ethics is not terribly complicated in theory. What I've found is that most of the anxiety people feel happens when they don't know what to do. Once they make a decision and live with it they are often able to regain confidence and move forward. So having a plan to make ethical decisions, particularly in regards to relationships, can provide enormous relief.

In the simplest terms the basic assumption of ethical relationships is that everyone begins with total **autonomy**, the ability to control what happens to them. Every decision should be made to preserve as much

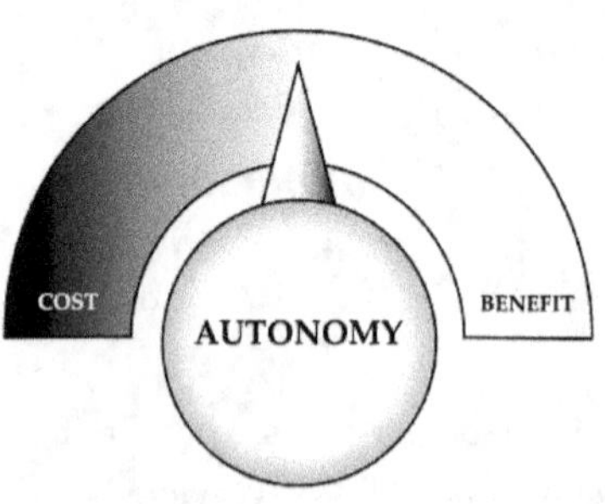

autonomy as possible for each individual. An easy way to remember the formula is to remember the letters **A-B-C**. The decision of one person to take away any amount of another person's **autonomy (A)** should be determined by considering the balance between the **benefit (B)**, and the **cost (C)** associated with the decision.

If a person is wanting to kill themselves or someone else, the cost of letting them do so far outweighs the benefit. Taking away their freedom to cause harm is ethically justified. They lose their right to autonomy as long as they are a threat to themselves or others.

Although this is a stark example it makes a clear point about how a situation could be examined from an ethical perspective. Hopefully you will never have to make this type of decision. But there are other difficult examples that could happen in your life.

What if your alcoholic child is asking you for money to pay the rent? You are aware that they have spent their paycheck on booze, and now they want you to rescue them from the dilemma they have created. In order to have an ethical relationship you will have to start with the assumption that they have the autonomy to drink as much as they want. You have the autonomy to decide whether to give them any money, but if you don't they may end up homeless. The short term benefit of paying their rent may be outweighed by the long term cost of your child remaining addicted and dependent.

Ethics is not about finding the perfect solution to every problem, but providing a strategy to determine the "rightest" choice that allows you to live with integrity and authenticity. Whatever choice you make, you must be willing to accept that integrity is expensive and requires you to bear the burden of living within your values. Consider also that the cost of abandoning your values may be much higher and greatly outweigh the benefit of being true to yourself.

In the end the real problem with people is that you are one of them. Eventually you will realize that you don't actually have a choice about having a relationship with someone. You have a relationship with every other human being on the planet in some way or another. They may not be close to you geographically, or connected to you by ethnicity, or culture, or personal beliefs. But you do have a choice to make about the quality of your relationship with everyone you encounter in your life—a choice that makes a meaningful difference in the way you see yourself.

A Universal Theory Of Relationships

When I started working with couples I realized there are a lot of approaches to repairing a damaged relationship. Sitting with two people who are looking to me for answers in the midst of a crisis can be intimidating. With so much at stake I wanted to offer the best possible support and guidance.

I explored many resources to learn the most effective methods backed by research and results. I found lots of really great information about what couples need to be successful at growing a healthy, resilient relationship that can withstand a lifetime of challenges.

But there was too much information. Although these ideas were helpful to me as a therapist, there was usually too much for the couple to implement in their daily lives. The deluge of books and websites and seminars was overwhelming for people who also had to go to work, raise kids, and buy groceries. What they needed was something simple and clear to fall back on when they were exhausted and not in the mood to be good at loving each other.

What I discovered was a simple explanation from research done by anthropologists who had studied the brains of couples in long-term happy relationships.[27] Their results identified three essential skills needed to make relationships work; essentially a universal theory of how to get along with each other.

It was certainly helpful for couples who appreciated the clear, practical advice. I soon realized that these skills were not only effective for couples but for all types of relationships. They are useful with families, friends, coworkers and anyone wanting to be much more successful at living with other people.

I also realized that within this framework people could learn how to be more ethical. Since the skills depend on your own efforts regardless of how other people behave, they inherently promote autonomy, compassion, and authenticity all at the same time.

Emotional Control – Researchers found that happy relationships depend on the ability of each person to take responsibility for their own emotions and stress levels. From an ethical point of view this means you no longer outsource your emotions to other people. Instead you recognize that expecting other people to make you happy, or blaming them for making you unhappy, is actually a form of manipulation.

You may attempt to control other people by expecting them to act differently in order to resolve your anxieties. And when they don't meet your expectations you can be tempted to make them responsible for how you feel, thinking of yourself as a victim who is being harmed in some way. This interferes with your own process of building resiliency and confidence.

Letting go of this habit may feel like a sign of weakness until you realize that it is an opportunity to accept your own limitations and free yourself from unrealistic expectations. When you take responsibility for your own emotions your energies can be focused more effectively on living out your values with authenticity.

Empathy – A second critical area of the brain that activates in happy relationships is associated with empathy. This correlates with what we know about mirror neurons that allow you to actually experience the emotions you observe in others. Tapping into this skill will upgrade your ability to accept a person's autonomy without feeling threatened.

One of the greatest obstacles in managing conflict is when you make it personal, or take it personal. This can quickly breed contempt and focus on WHO the person is instead of HOW they're acting. Experts agree that this kind of thinking makes it nearly impossible to repair the damage in a relationship.[28]

In an ethical relationship there is no room for defensiveness. If you accept that each person has the autonomy of their own feelings there is no need to defend yourself, or to convince someone they are wrong. Resisting the impulse to defend yourself may feel like a huge risk. As you become more authentic you will realize that all of the time you are wasting on seeking their approval could be spent seeking a solution instead.

Positive Illusions – The third area of the brain associated with happy relationships is connected to an ability to overlook attributes in the other person that you don't like and focus on their positive qualities. Initially this seems counterintuitive since some positive illusions about yourself and others can be naïve at best or potentially dangerous at their worst.

By choosing positive illusions you are not ignorant of the things you don't like. You are simply making a choice about where you place your attention. The trick is to be intentional rather than delusional when it comes to choosing your focus. If you are looking for negative qualities you will certainly find them and they will distract you from the positive qualities you want to accentuate.

Remember that you can only forgive others to the extent that you can forgive yourself. Whenever you feel overwhelmed with anger or resentment towards someone who bothers you, chances are you are grieving the illusion of control you wish you had over them. Choosing to accept them for who they are and even working towards appreciating them, will liberate you from this burden.

The real skill in positive illusions is learning how to recognize the strength behind every weakness. A lifetime of practice may be necessary to achieve this level of discernment. But it begins with learning to look with confidence and compassion at your own reflection shining back from the people around you every day.

Start Acting Healthy

As you contemplate how to respond to these ideas I strongly encourage you to give yourself a break. Looking at yourself from the inside out can be enormously painful and take many years to reach even a glimpse of wholeness. The search for authenticity is as complicated and confusing as it is rewarding.

Just when you think you've got yourself figured out, something pops up that surprises you. You might say or do something unexpected and wonder where that impulse came from. You might find yourself drawn to some person or new interest that you never expected. Or you might find that something you used to care deeply about no longer seems important anymore.

As you continue this pursuit of a more authentic life you will have to make an assessment of the relationships you have in your life. To be more precise you will have to make an assessment of HOW you have relationships in your life. As an authentic person you will become more and more aware of how valuable other people can be in helping you face your own insecurities and clarify your values.

The greatest challenge will come from people who make you feel the most uncomfortable. Each interaction has the potential for growth if you are willing to step up and face it. It's not possible to become more resilient without a certain amount of discomfort. The truth is you are already suffering in some way or another. Living with people is unavoidable and managing conflict with others is difficult. The real question is what are you getting out of all your efforts.

It's not unlike a guy who goes to the gym wanting to get healthier. If he is already out of shape he is already struggling with the cost of his lifestyle. Being unhealthy is already uncomfortable. So getting fit is really just a matter of shifting his discomfort to something that will get him more positive results.

The only way for him to get healthy is to start acting healthy. He will have to stop doing the things that unhealthy people do and start doing the things that healthy people do. If he goes to the gym and just stands in front of the treadmill, nothing about his health will actually change. He will have to get on the treadmill and do the work in order to get what he wants.

Learning how to maximize the return on your relationships takes a lot of work that can cause a lot of discomfort. Just like any exercise you will probably wake up the next day with sore muscles. In the case of authenticity this could look like varying degrees of identity crisis or emotional burnout.

Try not to let yourself get discouraged when you encounter a few setbacks. Use your skills of resiliency to recover and strengthen your emotional immunity. Seek support from other authentic people who will encourage you and role model healthy living. Make a point to track your progress and remind yourself how far you've come in building an authentic life. Set goals to be consistent in your practice and give yourself permission to take a break when you need it.

The truth is you are already suffering in some way or another. The real question is what are you getting out of all your efforts.

Above all learn to see that your search for authenticity is not just for your own benefit. As you live with integrity you are serving as a meaningful example for others to grow as well. This not only includes the people who admire you, but people who don't like you as well.

Your authenticity is necessary for all people to face their own insecurities. Whether you realize it or not you are a mirror to others reflecting back to them the aspects of themselves they need to address. By being authentic you are giving them the best possible chance of becoming healthy. Learning to claim your own autonomy with humility and integrity is the most ethical way to live an authentic life.

CHAPTER 5 NOTES

[22] Jung, C. G., & Jaffe, A. (1989). Memories, dreams, reflections: Recorded and edited by Aniela Jaffe ; translated from the German by Richard and Clara Winston. New York: Vintage. p.246

[23] Keysers, C., & Gazzola, V. (January 01, 2010). Social neuroscience: mirror neurons recorded in humans. *Current Biology : Cb, 20,* 8, 353-4.

[24] European Society of Human Genetics. (2009, May 25). Opposites Attract: How Genetics Influences Humans To Choose Their Mates. *ScienceDaily*. Retrieved from www.sciencedaily.com/releases/2009/05/090525105435.htm

[25] O'Keeffe, G. S., Clarke-Pearson, K., Mulligan, D. A., Altmann, T. R., Brown, A., Christakis, D. A., Falik, H. L., ... Nelson, K. G. (April 01, 2011). Clinical report - The impact of social media on children, adolescents, and families. *Pediatrics, 127,* 4, 800-804.

[26] Primack, B. A., Shensa, A., Sidani, J. E., Whaite, E. O., Lin, L. Y., Rosen, D., Colditz, J. B., ... Miller, E. (January 01, 2017). Social Media Use and Perceived Social Isolation Among Young Adults in the U.S. *American Journal of Preventive Medicine, 53,* 1, 1-8.

[27] Fisher, H. E. (2017). Anatomy of love: A natural history of mating, marriage, and why we stray.

[28] Gottman, J. M., & Silver, N. (2018). The seven principles for making marriage work.

Summary

- Relationships are essential in helping humans develop an individual identity.

- Mirror neurons assist humans in learning from others and connecting with each other emotionally.

- Ethical relationships strive to respect each person's autonomy while managing costs and benefits.

- Taking responsibility for your own emotions, showing empathy, and choosing to focus on positive traits will help you have more meaningful relationships.

- In order to live more authentically you must learn to see relationships as a tool for clarifying your values.

Reflections

1. What personality traits bother you the most when you see them in others? What personality traits do you find the most attractive?

2. How has your ability or inability to feel empathy been an asset or a burden?

3. What areas of your own autonomy do you find it difficult to hold onto when you have conflict in your relationships?

4. Think of your three most important relationships and name at least one thing that you find most valuable for each of them.

5. Which of your relationships will be the most effected when you begin to live your values with more integrity?

6 - AUTHENTIC LIVING
THE ART OF ALLOWING

In Chicago the Second City comedy club has been one of the most prolific producers of talented and influential comedians for generations. Since 1959 they have launched the careers of countless celebrities who have gone on to earn billions of dollars and shape our mainstream culture. At the core of this historic organization is a commitment to recruiting and training actors in the art of live improvisational comedy.

It has been said that one of the greatest fears most people will ever face is the prospect of public speaking. In improvisational comedy this fear is magnified by the fact that the actors have to perform without a script, and they have to make it funny at the same time.

In order to train for this type of performance actors spend years practicing techniques that help them respond to each other in ways that keep the action flowing as if it were planned all along. The courage it takes to stand up in front of a live audience with no idea what is about to happen has been described as somewhat equivalent to jumping out of an airplane.

That's why the actors work so hard to learn the rules of improvisation. Instead of merely winging it they have a set of guidelines to help them make decisions about HOW to act even when they have no idea WHAT is about to happen. In the midst of uncertainty and potential chaos the actors guide the audience through a story with confidence. In return the audience enjoys the perceived risks even more because they have to trust the actors to come up with something entertaining on the spot.

Perhaps the most important rule of improvisation is the concept of **"Yes...and."** This phrase embodies a mindset that promotes action throughout a scene so the story can keep moving without any interference. A typical example would be an actor who walks on stage pretending to carry an object. Once the actor says what the object is, all the other actors not only agree to that but add to it as well.

So if an actor walks on stage and says he is carrying a chicken, another actor may walk on stage also carrying a chicken. Or she may be carrying a bucket of chicken instead. Or to make it funnier she may pretend to be a chicken carrying a tiny person. In each case the original idea leads to something more than expected. The skill of the actors helps them create a work of art because they are able to build something original and intriguing by collaborating and allowing each other to contribute to the scene.

If either of them were to reject the contribution of the other actor the scene would be less believable. If the second actor tries to argue with the first actor that he is not carrying a chicken the audience would likely become confused or distracted from the story and the whole thing would be much less entertaining.

As you might expect the rules of improvisational comedy have applications far beyond the stage.[29] Leaders in every area of industry have studied the art form to improve their processes. The ability to face uncertainty with confidence promises enormous opportunities to innovate and expand possibilities into unchartered territory beyond the status quo. For our purposes we can use improvisational comedy as a metaphor to unlock a much deeper understanding of our authentic selves.

The Rules of Play

What people enjoy about improvisational comedy is that it mimics many of the components of child's play. It is a structured experience that is inherently creative and a little dangerous that both the actors and the audience can enjoy together.

Adults may be tempted to dismiss the importance of play in the life of a child. What might look like a silly waste of time, or maybe a bit of stress relief, is really a vital part of a child's physical, intellectual, and emotional growth. Researchers who have studied play have identified the developmental and therapeutic benefits that playtime can provide. In fact, play is so powerful doctors are being encouraged to prescribe play as part of a treatment program for children who are struggling with stress and other mental health issues.[30]

It's easy to see that a young child is unable to talk about their feelings when they can barely understand complex ideas, especially when they may be recovering from trauma or abuse. In order to help children manage their emotions practitioners of play therapy tap into a child's innate instincts to use symbolic items such as toys, costumes, and other objects specifically chosen for therapeutic expression in managing their subconscious anxieties.[31]

Although the play therapist may be able to recognize behavioral patterns, it is not entirely necessary for the professional or the child to even comprehend how the process of play is working. Ultimately the act of play itself is the therapy, with no need for interpretation or analysis to make it effective.

What this tells us is that play is an expression of the process used by our emotional immune system to make sense of the many unresolved anxieties lingering in our unconscious mind. Although play is typically considered a childish activity, there is no reason to assume that it doesn't work for adults as well. We can see how the symbolic nature of play can be translated into many other activities adults use in their daily lives to process their emotional experiences.

Although play is typically considered a childish activity, there is no reason to assume that it doesn't work for adults as well.

Take for example what we have learned about the psychological benefits of dreaming. As we sleep we experience a series of confusing and sometimes disturbing images. We usually have no idea what dreams mean, yet we instinctively know they are a symbolic representation of our subconscious mind. It isn't necessary to understand how dreaming works for it to work. What scientists do know is that it's a vital function of the brain's natural process of tidying up. Evidence suggests that all of those weird dreams are the result of our brain sorting out which memories to keep and which ones to get rid of.[32]

Consider also the power of storytelling as a medium of sharing ideas in a complex and subconscious way. Billions of dollars are spent around the world on books, movies, theater and music to express our internal conflicts in creative and intriguing ways.

The same is true of the global sports industry that encourages athletes from fledgling toddlers to elite professionals to represent their team, or their league, or their city, or their country by doing something better than somebody else. They wear costumes with logos surrounded by spectators who enthusiastically identify with them, cheering for their success. What could be more symbolic and cathartic than that?

In our own lives we struggle to make sense of consumer culture in order to conform or differentiate ourselves with this acquisition or that status symbol. Our ability to navigate the complex world of social symbolism can make a huge impact on our sense of self as we try to fit into or differentiate from whatever demographic we have been labeled with.

What does this have to do with our search for a more authentic life?

The big idea here is that the same benefits of symbolic play that helped us as children can help us as adults. The subconscious need to solve our sense of self is an integral part of living a more authentic life. Even though we are all grown up it makes sense that we should hack into our own healing process to maximize the benefits of play.

What Counts As Play

A study to examine the impact of play on children determined a link between different kinds of play and a child's development of critical thinking and self-control. Although many children are given endless opportunities to participate in sports, art classes, and other structured activities, researchers were able to show that children who were given time to engage in unstructured play were more capable of setting their own goals and regulating their own emotions.[33]

The take away is that not all types of play are beneficial in the same way. In structured play children are typically guided by adults with an agenda focused on a predetermined goal. This type of play is inherently limited by time, resources, and rules that hinder or even forbid creative problem solving and unregulated peer interaction.

If the intention is to help children develop resiliency, they must be given opportunities to play on their own terms. Unstructured play has fewer time constraints, provides access to open spaces and materials for creative expression, and offers opportunities for children to engage in their own social interactions that may lead to conflict and difficult emotions. This type of play is often messy and unpredictable, appearing to be pointless and sometimes annoying to adults who underestimate the importance of these troublesome experiences.

What happens is that adults concerned about a child will monitor play in order to sanitize and control it. Allowing children to make messes and mistakes can be risky. Adults who are unable to recognize the value of unstructured play are probably unable to trust their own emotional immune system for healing and growth. In my work it is common for adults to resist the idea that they can benefit from play just like children.

They immediately envision themselves having a tea party with dolls and tiny dishes, or they imagine a game of pretend where they dress up as superheroes or pirates on an adventure. Although this would be perfectly effective as a therapeutic activity, it is not exactly what I have in mind. What I really mean is that adults wanting to access the benefits of unstructured play can begin by practicing **playfulness**.

In the adult world there are multitudes of situations that are obviously too serious to be taken with a lighthearted approach. From personal concerns about health, finances and family conflict, to larger issues of social and cultural challenges, adults can easily feel overwhelmed with their responsibilities. The thought of being playful about serious issues can seem offensive.

Adults can practice play and playfulness in order to resolve conscious and subconscious inner conflicts.

As a therapist I would never suggest that a client have a playful attitude about cancer. There is also nothing lighthearted about processing childhood abuse or mood disorders. It can't be stated too firmly that this idea has nothing to do with minimizing or ignoring serious concerns. The suggestion to foster a playful mindset is really about accessing the power of play to serve as a stand in for emotional burdens we can't face otherwise.

When children play they are managing difficult emotions equivalent to the ones faced by adults. They may have witnessed domestic violence, be processing grief over a lost family member, or feeling overwhelmed with so many adult expectations. Whatever psychological distress they don't know how to handle in the real world they process subconsciously through play with symbolic objects and activities that represent the anxieties they are otherwise unable to resolve.

In the same way, adults can practice play and playfulness in order to resolve conscious and subconscious inner conflicts that linger from the daily grind of living their values with integrity. By intentionally incorporating the qualities of genuine play into your life, either as an activity you schedule on your calendar, or as a mindset you apply to all areas of your daily life, you can move towards a more practical understanding and expression of your authentic self.

But it must be the real thing. In order for play to work well as a tool for authentic living it must include certain elements identified by experts in the field of education.[34] The irony of this is that because **authentic play** is unstructured, it's' generally impossible to define it and design it to meet any strict criteria. That would defeat the purpose altogether. Instead these are descriptions of the mental attitude needed to make any activity, no matter how mundane, into a playful experience.

Play is self-directed. The word freedom gets tossed around by people who are concerned over how much control they have or don't have in any given situation. Your own definition of freedom can be an indicator of your ability to find happiness and to live an authentic life. When you learn to see freedom as a state of mind you can dismantle much of the anxiety about controlling others and their control over you.

Even activities that are supposed to be fun can quickly feel like a chore if they are mandated by some authority figure. Children engaged in self-directed play are enthusiastic about the activity because they are in control of what they do and how they do it, or even if they do it all. Adults who feel like their entire lives are imposed upon them will consistently find themselves struggling with burnout, depression, and resentment. So what can they do if they are feeling trapped in a tedious job, an unsatisfying relationship, or other regrettable dilemma?

Adopting a playful mindset means learning how to reframe your situation as something you GET to do rather than something you HAVE to do. This shift in thinking allows you to tap into a recognition of the abundance and freedom to not only choose WHAT you are doing, but HOW you are doing it. Ask yourself how well the current situation promotes your values. Even if you can't change the situation you can at least change your reason for doing it. Either way you can recalibrate the experience into something that supports who you want to be.

Play has intrinsic value. You will need to analyze WHY you are doing something to stay authentically motivated. Activities that have extrinsic value are those which produce results not connected to the activity itself. Activities that have intrinsic value are those that you can enjoy merely for the pleasure of the experience.

If a child enjoys painting a picture they will find it much less rewarding knowing they have to sell it when they are done. Once the purpose is not just about painting, the playfulness of something they love turns into work. It would be like thinking that the purpose of dancing is to get to the other end of the stage as fast as possible. The real pleasure of dancing comes from all of the other steps in between.

Conventional wisdom has already taught us that the most successful people are those who make a living doing something they would gladly do for free. Even the most unpleasant activity has the potential to be its own reward if you are able to approach it with an authentic attitude. The practice of mindfulness can make an enormous difference by training you to notice the aspects of your work that bring satisfaction.

Play is constructive. Watch a child playing with blocks and you will see a mind at work. Whether they are building something, taking something apart, pretending to be a princess, or trying to hit a target, all of their attention is focused on achieving a goal. If they choose to make rules for their game it is clear that they are still in charge and can change the rules at any time.

This aspect of play has much to do with an instinctive drive to solve problems. In the case of play they are problems a child has invented for themselves. Adults may not realize it but they do the same thing. Everything from crossword puzzles to climate change can be ways to occupy their need to assert some sense of control over the world.

Pay attention to the problems you create for yourself. How many of the challenges you face each day, and the emotional toll that comes with them, are actually self-imposed? If your life feels complicated there's a good chance you are the one complicating it. When you adopt a playful attitude you give yourself permission to rewrite the rules of your life so you can enjoy being the person you want to be.

Play is creative. In light of the symbolic nature of play it makes sense that it must involve some degree of imagination. Authentic play allows children to create new realties and try out different identities in a make believe world. There may be no better way to access the healing power of the subconscious than through creative activities that allow us to make something new, follow a gut feeling, or develop an innovative idea.

The essence of creativity is reaffirming your power to make changes in your life and have a sense of control in an unpredictable world. Everything that becomes real must first be formed in your imagination. The attitude of playfulness opens up your mind to possibilities about who you can be and how to make that vision come true.

But it can't happen when you are second guessing yourself and worrying about making mistakes. For the creative process to work you will have to become comfortable with messiness and uncertainty. Whether you are pursuing a creative project or pursuing a project creatively, a playful mindset gives you an opportunity to practice listening to your inner voice and trusting your intuition. These efforts will strengthen your resiliency and resolve so that you can respond to every crisis – real or imagined – with confidence.

Play is a little dangerous. Imagine the excitement children feel from a simple game of chase. One child runs away afraid of getting caught, the other runs close behind trying to outsmart them. They both know there is no real danger, but the experience is just as exhilarating. By fabricating **synthetic danger** children are able to generate a feeling of alert attention that incorporates all the aspects of play in a way that is satisfying and empowering.

Video game designers are aware that the virtual worlds they create allow players to fail over and over again with no real world consequences.[35] In order for play to be authentic it must include some type of perceived risk blended with an underlying sense of safety. These ingredients combine to produce a "flow" state where a child can confront their vulnerability subconsciously and address unresolved insecurities successfully.

As an adult you may not realize you are doing the same thing on a grander scale. Alongside recreational activities that simulate a feeling of danger, you likely infuse your life with manufactured challenges to increase your sense of risk. How important is it really to have yard of the month? Or be able to make a souffle? In the big scheme of things failing at these endeavors won't change your life, but the experience will likely satisfy other subconscious needs. Intentionally taking some healthy risks and pretending to slay a few dragons can be a playful way to cope with the real anxieties of adulthood.

How To Play Like A Grown-Up

There is a lot of talk about self-care in the media and just as many ways to explain how it is done. Any blog post or news report about self-care almost always displays images of people getting a massage or doing yoga on a mountaintop. Those things are certainly appealing and can be part of a healthy lifestyle. But really taking care of your "self" involves a much more comprehensive effort to restructure your life.

For most people the process will need to include some far less comfortable activities. True self-care may require you to complete unpleasant tasks like cleaning out your garage, or writing your will. It may mean ending relationships with toxic people or looking for a new job. Or it might mean finally committing to the process of therapy.

Just because these things are difficult it certainly doesn't mean they should be avoided. They may be necessary to help you genuinely care for the person you really want to be. Until you really buckle down and make some difficult decisions about how you live your real life, all of the money you spend on spa treatments and island vacations may be wasted.

Be careful not to confuse play with relaxation. Authentic play is not passive but intentional. When you make this mistake you may be merely procrastinating instead. Play is not intended to distract you from the challenges of adulthood but to make them more bearable, and even more enjoyable. This makes a huge difference in how effective play can be as a healing tool.

Adding play to your life is good, but what we are looking for is an overall mindset of playfulness. The difference is significant because it's not just about changing what you do but changing how you see yourself as a person. Tell yourself that you are not just a person who plays, but you are a playful person. This works much better if you learn to incorporate it into your life rather than simply scheduling it as an event on your calendar. In fact it might help to do it backwards.

Take the calendar you already have and analyze it through the lens of authentic play. How much of what you already do is self-directed? What activities do you actually enjoy for their own sake? When do you have opportunities to build something or use your imagination? Who is in charge of the risks and challenges you take each day? If you discover that your life is missing the ingredients of authentic play it might explain why you feel like an adult all the time.

When children play it comes natural to them. It isn't something they have to learn how to do. We might assume that some activities are specifically play, and other activities are not play. But from an emotional standpoint everything they do is infused with the spirit of play in some way or another.

For children even things like eating and getting dressed have a playfulness that satisfies their curiosity. Something as simple as walking from one place to another is an opportunity to pretend or invent a new challenge. Every object they touch has the potential to be a puppet, or a sword, or an airplane.

Adults see these traits as charming in children but embarrassing for themselves. If you see another adult pretending to be a wizard or a princess it might feel awkward. You would probably wonder if they are a little crazy unless they are getting paid for it, or actually playing with a child. Then for some reason it's perfectly acceptable.

Am I suggesting you show up at work dressed as a superhero? It's certainly fun to imagine. Just considering it might be enough to engage your subconscious, because your brain wants you to play. It's always looking for opportunities to process those unresolved anxieties you've been holding onto for however long… maybe even since childhood.

The fact is you are already practicing play in your life in ways you aren't aware. It happens all the time. Just like children we intuitively use symbolic meaning to substitute regular activities and everyday items to process inner conflicts and repressed insecurities. Everything from the clothes you wear and the car you drive to the social and political causes that motivate you, tells a hidden story about the person you are trying to be.

The problem comes when you take too seriously the things in your life that are really only meant for play. When this happens you can lose the benefit of playfulness and end up with more stress and unresolved anxieties than you started with. By learning to identify the quality of play in your life you can upgrade the impact it has on your ability to live an authentic life.

Take a look at these activities you are probably using to satisfy your subconscious needs, and consider how you can incorporate a more playful mindset.

Creativity – If you've ever stood in front of a famous piece of art and thought maybe you could have painted something like that you have experienced the spirit of play. Any form of creativity that inspires you to express yourself is calling you to be more authentic. Rather than standing there looking at what others have done, overcome your fear of failure and go make something yourself. This may be expressed through cooking, fashion, or writing a book. Allow yourself to wander into uncharted territory and try a new skill that you can enjoy for the sheer pleasure of it.

Shopping – Have you ever looked at another person's shopping cart and wondered what it says about their life? Now take a look at your own cart and ask yourself what does it say about you. In the modern marketplace almost everything you buy is designed to influence consumer behavior by appealing to your self-image. As long as you don't fall for it hook, line, and sinker, you can use these things to set the stage for an authentic performance, with you as the star. Just remember that they don't define you as a person. They are merely props in a drama you are writing from the inside out.

Entertainment – The best comedians make us laugh about topics that are uncomfortable. The best movies explore ideas and make us question our assumptions. Our favorite music helps us access deeply felt emotions. All of these activities may seem like ways to pass the time, but the real purpose of entertainment is to help us reflect on our inner selves in a safe and meaningful way. Use entertainment more intentionally to manage anxieties and increase emotional awareness.

Sports – There's a reason watching your local team gets you so excited, or disappointed as the case may be. Those emotions are connecting you to the power of play even though you are on the sidelines. Artificial rivalries are fun, but if you really want the benefit of play participate in self-directed activities like athletics, video games, dancing, hiking or yoga that let you engage your mind and body more fully in the process of play.

Socialization – It's easier to connect with more people than at any time in history and yet the perils of social networking can make it a mixed blessing. By design social media diminishes the authenticity of those who take it too seriously. Use it in a playful way to express yourself without getting pulled in to so much superficial drama. Look for friends who share your intention to embrace a playful spirit. Along with your virtual friends make a point to actually be in the room with those who are already good at authentic play, including children and animals, the original masters of authenticity.

Therapy – Taking time out to process difficult emotions with a therapist may not be considered particularly playful but all of the ingredients are there. Effective therapy allows a client to be self-directed, is intrinsically rewarding, and offers opportunities for problem solving and creative thinking. Above all it allows a client to take risks in a safe environment as they practice healthy emotional responses to real world concerns.

Embracing Vulnerability

In a conversation with a client about his fear of flying we uncovered some new insights about vulnerability. After searching online and crunching the numbers we determined that there are over one million flights per day around the world totaling nearly 40 million flights per year. Most estimates place the odds of dying in a plane crash at about 1 in 5 million[36]. Even so, he said the statistics didn't really help him feel better.

When we dug a little deeper he admitted the real issue was not his fear of dying on a plane, but his fear of dying at all. He said it bothered him that he might die and miss out on so many things that he still wanted to do with his life. What he was actually afraid of was the awareness of his vulnerability.

I pointed out to him that it's the same vulnerability he lives with on the ground, driving in his car, going to the mall, and living his daily life. Even when he sees bad things happen to people with random misfortune he is able to maintain a level of functional courage. Maybe being on a plane doesn't actually make him more vulnerable, it just magnifies his vulnerability and makes it harder to ignore.

The relationship between vulnerability and authenticity is integral. You cannot have one without the other. Wanting to be in control of your life may feel completely ordinary, but any amount of denial or ignorance about the fact of your vulnerability will increase your potential for disillusionment and grief over the loss of some outcome that you've imagined for yourself. An essential ingredient of authenticity is your ever increasing awareness about what you can and can't control.

> *The relationship between vulnerability and authenticity is integral. You cannot have one without the other.*

I'll admit this line of reasoning can lead to a feeling of despair. Why even bother if you don't have control over what happens to you? Many people have asked the same question, and the best response I have found is that freedom is on the other side of despair.

The fact that you can even ask that question means you also have the freedom to find your own answers. Obviously you should pay your bills, and take care of your health, and drive safely, and lock your doors at night. All of those choices are things you can actually control. But even if you eat your vegetables and act like a grown up bad things may still happen. Choosing to be responsible in the face of your vulnerability isn't a waste of time. It's the foundation for the freedom to live an authentic life.

If you spend time with children you can learn a lot about the relationship between vulnerability and authenticity. From the day they are born they have no choice but to comply with the expectations of adults. For the first few years they spend their days at the direction of others. What they eat, what they wear, where they go, and many other choices are made for them.

All the while children are inherently capable of finding opportunities to be playful, curious, and compassionate in the midst of their vulnerability. Along with their unfiltered perspective they are naturally energetic, expressive, intuitive and full of wonder. They display a remarkable acceptance of their subordinate status while maintaining an enthusiasm for life.

That degree of authenticity, the kind you experienced in childhood, can seem simultaneously familiar and elusive. When you see it in children you may experience a mix of emotions. You long for the innocent optimism of youth while acknowledging the endless responsibilities that come with adult privileges.

Nurturing authenticity requires a willingness to accept life as a paradox. It means adopting a mindset that skillfully integrates both vulnerability and authenticity like the child you used to be. It means striving to be an adult who can tap into your childhood instinct for allowing life to happen around you without apology or cynicism.

If this seems unsettling or impossible you may be convinced that being an adult is serious business that requires being serious about serious things. You may have spent so much time being a firefighter that you don't know how to let your guard down and enjoy the life you have been working so hard to protect. But if you see life as nothing more than a series of burning buildings, you will live in a constant state of emergency.

The first step to changing this mindset is to ask who is starting all the fires. It's true that other people might light fires in their life and expect you to put them out. But their emergency does not always have to be your emergency. That kind of drama is the result of your own expectations about who you are supposed to be, and how you are supposed to act.

Remember that every dilemma in your life is a reflection of your own values. You are the one who chooses which boulders to push up the hill. Accepting your limits will help you focus your attention on the fires that are truly worth fighting.

In order to live a truly authentic life you must discover that you are the one writing the story. You are the one who chooses which mask to wear. You are the one who decides what it takes to be the hero of your own adventure. Once you reach this understanding you will experience a monumental shift in your perspective.

Not every situation you experience requires so much intensity and distress. The practice of playfulness gives you skills and insight to face your vulnerability without losing your confidence. In the beginning it will seem impossible to reframe your emergencies in a playful way. How can you be playful about paying the rent? What is so charming about managing your heart disease? Who in their right mind would view traffic as synthetic danger?

As an adult you are convinced of the gravity in each of these dilemmas. The potential risks may seem overwhelming. But that doesn't mean you can't approach them with the ingredients of play. If you can't pay the rent you might need to find a creative and fun way to save money. What better way to improve your health than playing with your grandchildren. Getting out of traffic and finding an alternate route can lead to new discoveries.

In every case you can accept your vulnerability while refusing to be burdened by it. That doesn't mean it will be easy. Learning to play is always a little messy and often it could seem like a waste of time. You might try something new and it is an utter failure. Even so, the very act of reclaiming your authenticity in the face of your vulnerability will upgrade your sense of meaning and fulfillment.

Take a look around and ask yourself if there are really so many burning buildings in your life. Begin to practice play as a way to liberate yourself from a life of urgency and worry. Pledge to move as many areas of your life from one category to the other. Over time you will learn to see that most of the burning buildings are really opportunities to rediscover your authenticity.

The Power of AND

Lying on a massage table and having someone apply pressure to your muscles and joints is typically seen as a positive experience. With an expert massage therapist you can often feel immediate relief from pain and soreness caused by injury, vigorous activity, or anxiety lingering in your body. Although the experience itself is relaxing the process of massage is actually using your own pain as a part of the procedure.

The techniques used in massage rely on a curious reaction that your body has to discomfort. When muscles and joints are pushed beyond their limits they have a natural healing process designed to repair millions of microscopic tears in the tissue that happen during exercise or exertion. As muscles attempt to strengthen the damaged area with additional tissue they can become tense or swollen.

Whenever this healing process gets out of hand the muscles might overcompensate causing the body to function poorly. The primary strategy to relieve the swelling that builds up is to manipulate the affected area in order to help it relax. Chemical reactions caused by the sensation of touch and pressure affect the electrical signals being sent by the nerves to the muscles and skin.

In trigger point massage this can be a particularly dramatic experience. The massage therapist works with the client to identify a specific area of discomfort that triggers pain signals in other areas of the body. She then applies pressure to actually generate the pain response while the client breathes deeply, allowing the pain to radiate. Although this seems like the opposite way to heal pain, it's actually using the body's natural response to help it recover. Surprisingly, after a few seconds of allowing the pain it begins to fade and eventually subsides.

> *Rather than hiding from your pain you can choose to face it, feel it, and free yourself from it.*

Instead of avoiding the pain the idea behind trigger point massage is that the body's tension around the painful area is preventing it from relaxing and recovering. The act of triggering the pain and then intentionally allowing it to fade changes the way the nerves interpret the painful experience. By allowing the discomfort and breathing deeply the client is telling her body that it is no longer necessary to hold onto the pain.[37]

The art of allowing feels a lot like this. In all of life there are countless ways you may have decided that the pain you feel is necessary to protect you. You may have been pushed beyond your limits over and over again. You may have needed to shield yourself for a time resulting in emotional scar tissue that has built up. But the scar tissue is not meant to keep you from moving on. It is only there to make you more resilient. If you continue to stay anxious and tense you can never fully benefit from your own healing process. The healing will never be complete.

The practice of embracing your vulnerability gives you the insight and inspiration to face the contradiction of your pain. Rather than hiding from it you can choose to face it, feel it, and free yourself from it. Just like a massage therapist might push into the pain to help you alleviate it, the process of psychotherapy can help you identify and demystify the concerns that have been bothering you for years.

One of the most effective techniques I have used with clients to shift their thinking in this way is to change a very simple word in their vocabulary. Just like the actors who stand on the stage and say "Yes… and" in order to keep the action going, I ask them to replace the word BUT with AND in their language.

A typical statement from a client struggling with uncertainty places two ideas next to each other that seem to compete in their minds.

I want to be healthy, BUT I want to eat junk food.

My job is killing me, BUT I need to pay the bills.

We fight all the time, BUT we don't want a divorce.

All of these situations feel like a puzzle that can't be solved. By including the word BUT in the statement it automatically frames the crisis as a contradiction. Saying it this way, and thinking this way, makes it much less likely to get any results. It's like a roadblock to progress.

Choosing to replace the word BUT with AND can help change the framework entirely into a problem solving machine. Letting both of the ideas exist together allows them both to be true at the same time. Now they can appear as two separate possibilities that have their own merit and meaning.

I want to be healthy AND I want to eat junk food. Of course you want both of these things. Junk food is delicious. Being healthy is an important goal. Giving yourself permission to have both desires removes the unnecessary shame and opens up the possibility to make a more reasonable choice.

My job is killing me, AND I need to pay the bills. This reality challenges us all. Both ideas require a degree of humility. When they were in competition they felt like a curse. When they are accepted together they sound more like a signal for the need to make thoughtful changes.

We fight all the time, AND we don't want a divorce. When you look at these ideas together they highlight the urgency of the situation. Rather than framing them as a dilemma you can recognize the cause and effect and focus on the solution instead of the problem.

The power of AND is a first step in recognizing your authentic power to feel confident in the face of uncertainty. As you practice this technique and begin to work on the skills described in this book you can develop the confidence you need to stand on the stage without a script, or run into a burning building if the need arises.

Integrity – Removing your mask may be scary at first. But it's a crucial first step in clarifying your values. Behind that mask is someone longing to be accepted and loved fully. Choose to be the person who fills that need. Allow yourself to be a whole person who is willing to take charge of their values and live them with courage and integrity.

Resiliency – Sometimes you see the storm coming, and other times it catches you by surprise. Emotional immunity is built in to your authentic self and is able to get your through the next storm and all the storms to come. Instead of being afraid of your emotions, learn to see them as allies in your struggle toward healing. Allow your authentic emotions to protect you and lead you to a more fulfilling life.

Humility – At the top of the mountain you can see clearly the choice that needs to be made. On one side is the pile of boulders you let go of, and on the other is the chance for freedom. In order to get there you must embrace the humility needed to accept your limitations and live with gratitude and compassion. Humility is a fact. You can choose humility or it will be forced upon you. Allow the discomfort of humility to guide you toward authentic intentions that are genuinely meaningful and satisfying.

Autonomy – Let others be wrong. Let others be right. Allow yourself to be part of the healing that comes from living an authentic life. Not only are all of those people serving as a mirror for your own growth, you are a mirror to them. Authenticity is contagious. When some people catch it they feel better. When other people catch it they feel worse. The art of allowing gives you the skills you need to navigate the conflicts that come from everybody working on themselves in their own way.

Vulnerability – Not everything in life is a comedy. It can be full of drama and uncertainty. But not everything in life is a burning building. The art of allowing is embracing your vulnerability with the courage to be authentic regardless if it feels like a comedy or tragedy. Over time you may not even be able to tell the difference. The good news is that you don't have to know how it works for it to work. When it's all said and done all you really need to know is that life is too important to be taken seriously.

An Imperfect Book

Many months before this book was complete I found myself trapped in anxiety about how to write something that would be worth all the trouble. I had been sharing these ideas with each of my clients in our sessions and they proved to be helpful. It occurred to me that if I could just hand them a book with all of these ideas they could take it with them and maybe even share it with others.

I also realized it would give me the opportunity to help a significantly larger number of people who might benefit from my work as well. With a book I could educate and encourage a potentially unlimited number of readers and build a supportive community. I recognized that I could make much better use of my time by developing resources that could last much longer than a single session. So I began to write.

Almost immediately I became frozen with self-doubt. Who did I think I was trying to write a book about mental health? What if I wrote something inaccurate or couldn't explain it well? What if I faced criticism? What if I spent months writing and researching, editing and rewriting and it turned out awful? What if the whole thing ended up being a huge waste of time?

My self-doubt got the best of me. I stopped writing and convinced myself that it didn't matter if I wrote nothing at all. I already have a successful practice and I enjoy working with my clients. I don't owe anybody anything since nobody even knew I was writing it. I could just forget about the whole thing and just be happy.

And that's what I did for a few months. Even though I had written an outline and drafted a few paragraphs I became afraid that it would not be good enough. So I put it away and forgot about it. Every day I would go to work and do my job and go home satisfied with my day. This felt like enough. I knew I didn't have to do anything more to be happy.

But somewhere along the way I realized I was no longer happy. In fact I was getting depressed. On the outside I was very comfortable and should have been happy. But on the inside I wasn't. I was bored. As a therapist I decided to put myself on the other side of the couch. I knew from experience I needed to find a problem to solve or the problems would start to find me.

My anxiety about writing a book was an emotional dashboard light. It was telling me that I could no longer exist in my current state whether I admitted it or not. I knew I was needing to grow and writing this book was part of that growth. If I continued to ignore the dashboard light things would start getting worse. My repressed anxiety would eventually start causing problems for me through poor habits and laziness. I would eventually make mistakes and start sabotaging myself subconsciously. My depression was telling me that I was not living up to who I really wanted to be on the inside.

The other option was to choose my own problem to solve. And I already knew what that problem needed to be. Even if months of writing was a huge waste of time I could at least enjoy it while it lasted. I chose to approach it with a playful mindset. I decided to start writing again and to intentionally start writing poorly.

What I realized was that I was wanting to write a perfect book. I had imagined that it would be an epic timeless manifesto that would change the world. But when I decided to write an imperfect book all of the pressure went away. I still did my best, but I had to keep reminding myself that it didn't have to be better than my best. It just had to be good enough.

By letting go of my preconceived ideas about what it should be, I was able to allow the book to be what it is – an imperfect book.[38] Each day as I wrote I had some idea what was supposed to happen but along the way I got distracted. So I followed those distractions and listened to my intuition. If I became curious I gave myself permission to ask questions and look for the answers.

What could have been a drudgery turned into an adventure. Interesting ideas seemed to find me in surprising ways. A meme on the internet, a line from a movie, an article in the news, or something shared in a conversation all caught my attention and gave me an opportunity to explore. My need to control the outcome of this process proved to be pointless and frustrating. In the end I left a lot of things out. Were they a waste of time? By all means no. I enjoyed every minute of it.

My hope is that you can see I am trying to practice what I preach. Being authentic is messy and inconvenient and sometimes means you get depressed, anxious, frustrated, and have a crisis that you don't want anybody to know about. And then maybe you'll put it in a book that you aren't sure anyone will read.

I hope the same thing happens to you. I hope you have a crisis that makes you give up on being somebody you don't want to be. I hope you learn to appreciate that crisis and then go find a problem to solve that helps you be yourself. I hope you decide to stop trying to control the things you can't control and quit wanting to change the people who bother you. I hope you discover that you are vulnerable and precious like a child and that's okay.

I hope you never stop learning how to be clear and present and confident with who you are, ready for the next adventure.

CHAPTER 6 NOTES

[29] Fey, T. (2013). *Bossypants*. New York: Little, Brown.

[30] Yogman, M., Garner, A., Hutchinson, J., Hirsh-Pasek, K., & Golinkoff, R. M. (September 01, 2018). The Power of Play: A Pediatric Role in Enhancing Development in Young Children. *Pediatrics, 142,* 3.)

[31] Homeyer, L. E., & Morrison, M. O. (December 07, 2008). Play Therapy: Practice, Issues, and Trends. *American Journal of Play, 1,* 2, 210-228.

[32] Eichenlaub, J.-B., van, R. E., Gaskell, M. G., Lewis, P. A., Maby, E., Malinowski, J. E., Walker, M. P., ... Blagrove, M. (June 01, 2018). Incorporation of recent waking-life experiences in dreams correlates with frontal theta activity in REM sleep. *Social Cognitive and Affective Neuroscience, 13,* 6, 637-647.

[33] Jane Elizabeth Barker, Andrei D. Semenov, Laura Michaelson, Lindsay S. Provan, Hannah R. Snyder, & Yuko Munakata. (June 01, 2014). Less-structured time in children's daily lives predicts self-directed executive functioning. *Frontiers in Psychology, 5.*

[34] Gray, P. (2015). Free to learn: Why unleashing the instinct to play will make our children happier, more self-reliant, and better students for life.

[35] Films for the Humanities & Sciences (Firm), Films Media Group., & TED Conferences LLC. (2012). *TEDTalks: Jane McGonigal - Gaming Can Make a Better World.* New York, N.Y: Films Media Group.

[36] Shepardson, D. (2019, January 02). Fatalities on commercial passenger aircraft rise in 2018. Retrieved from https://www.reuters.com/article/us-airlines-safety-worldwide/fatalities-on-commercial-passenger-aircraft-rise-in-2018-idUSKCN1OW007

[37] Moayedi, M., & Davis, K. D. (January 01, 2013). Theories of pain: from specificity to gate control. *Journal of Neurophysiology, 109,* 1, 5-12.

[38] Pogosyan, M. (2017, January 2). The Beauty of Imperfection; the Japanese concept of wabi-sabi. Retrieved from https://www.psychologytoday.com/us/blog/between-cultures/201701/the-beauty-imperfection.

Summary

- Play is a natural response to coping with stress and unresolved subconscious anxieties.

- Adults can use play and playfulness to increase resiliency and confidence.

- Authentic play promotes a sense of empowerment while embracing vulnerability.

- Learning to allow the story to unfold will open up unlimited opportunities to discover your authentic self and live a more satisfying life.

Reflections

1. How often do you feel like you are standing on a stage without a script?

2. What are some symbolic objects in your everyday life that are likely attached to subconscious insecurities?

3. What aspects of your life that you take seriously may actually be an example of synthetic danger?

4. Name a typically unpleasant activity that you could make more enjoyable by incorporating a sense of playfulness.

5. How does thinking and living like an adult help or hinder your ability to experience authenticity?

7 - AUTHENTIC THINKING
LEARNING TO DANCE

When a professional ballerina dances it's a thing of beauty. Her graceful movements make her appear to float across the stage in perfect coordination with the music. Her body is a living piece of art that is utterly inspiring. At the peak of her performance she is nothing short of a miracle. Watching her dance it's easy to forget the extraordinary amount of suffering she has endured to reach that level of expertise.

As a tiny baby she began with no control over her limbs. Before long she learned to crawl, and then to walk, and then to run. Each new skill she gained along the way marked a greater degree of complexity in her development. Then one day she stepped onto the dance floor for the first time to learn another new set of skills along with many new ways to feel clumsy and frustrated.

Learning to walk and run are hard enough, but becoming a dancer requires a far more sophisticated level of concentration about how her body moves. In order to be more skillful she had to focus on changing old habits and practicing new ones. Such a goal cannot be achieved without endless perseverance and confidence. For every delicate pirouette there were a thousand stumbles to the floor.

When we think about making improvements we don't need to frame our old habits as being bad or good. It would be better to think of our habits and choices as more or less sophisticated. The word *sophistication* comes from the Greek word *sophia* meaning "wisdom or skill." The idea is that gaining new skills requires experience combined with understanding.

When a baby learns to walk we celebrate their progress. At each new stage we encourage her to take chances so she can experience what it feels like to do something new. When she bumps into the coffee table we don't make fun of her and tell her to quit trying. We cheer her on, and hold her hand telling her to try again because we know that one day she will be able to dance.

The same is true for you. As you learn to improve there is no benefit in feeling shame about your old habits. They were there for a reason. They played a part in helping you reach greater levels of sophistication in your path towards authenticity. Everybody has to learn how to crawl before they can walk.

The real goal of mental health is seeking a more sophisticated quality of thinking. Just like a dancer who repeats the same sequence of steps to commit them to memory, the work of therapy involves many repetitions of the same thought patterns that lead to a more positive outcome. When you study dance you are using your body to practice dancing. In therapy you are using your mind to practice thinking.

Learning to dance is awkward because you've never moved in quite that way before. You accept it because you know it takes practice to get better at it. The same is true when you start changing how you think. It's okay to suck at it for a while. It takes practice.

Consider these exercises as a type of mental health dance practice. They are opportunities to think about your own thinking in a way you've probably never done before. Instead of feeling bad about it choose to celebrate each tiny step you make. Most people don't work this hard unless they have to. A lot of people treat their mental health like they treat their dental health; they wait until something hurts before they get help.

Now is the time to change that pattern. Be proactive about getting skillful in your thinking. Work through these exercises in a way that benefits you. Take them one at a time and try them out. Share them with other people you can trust. One of the best ways to increase your own skill is to teach what you have learned to someone else.

You can sit and watch others dance all day but until you get up and start doing something you can't be a dancer. In order to live an authentic life you have to be intentional about doing what it takes to gain the skills.

Allow yourself to feel awkward. Listen to your emotions and let them do their work. Become aware of unresolved issues that need to be addressed. Make a commitment to follow through with them wherever they lead you. Choose to get help from qualified mental health practitioners who can assist you in learning how to take the next step.

Exercise #1:
Identifying Labels

Taking charge of your identity is one of the first steps toward becoming more authentic. You have to ask a lot of questions about yourself in order to get a clear understanding of who you are before you can be who you want to be. This exercise is designed to help you sort out the difference between what other people tell you about who you are, and what you truly think about yourself.

STEP 1: On a clean piece of paper draw a large circle about the size of your hand. On the outside of the circle write down some of the labels that other people have given you. Some of them might be positive (funny, smart, dependable, attractive). Some of them might be negative (grumpy, lazy, inconsiderate, ugly). And some of them might be neutral (male, Hispanic, parent, employee).

STEP 2: Now on the inside of the circle write down some of the labels you give yourself. They may also be positive, negative or neutral, and may be the same or different than the labels given to you by others.

STEP 3: Underline the labels you most want to change. Now ask yourself the following questions:

- What would it take to change the labels on the outside?
- Which of the labels on the outside do you feel powerless to change?
- Which of the labels on the inside do you have the most control over?
- What would it take to change the labels on the inside?

Whenever I have completed this exercise with many clients there are a few patterns that emerge.

First, most people have a few of the labels that match both the inside and the outside. It's important to realize that there is a mixed bag of feelings about who you are. Not all of these labels are bad things. And there are some labels that can't be changed. We know that labels are hardly an accurate picture of someone's true identity. This exercise is a good way to come to terms with the shadow aspects of our personality.

Second, usually the labels on the outside are much harder to do anything about. This is because there are so many people that have to be influenced to make a difference. And even if you could change a small number of people's opinions, that could change in an instant. This might help you recognize why you feel so overwhelmed with the task of managing your reputation.

Third, most people admit pretty quickly that the only labels they have any real control over are the ones on the inside. They may not all be pleasant to look at but at least they are realistic targets for self-improvement. Working from the inside out is hard work and requires a great deal of integrity. But the good news is if you work on the inside then the outside will take care of itself.

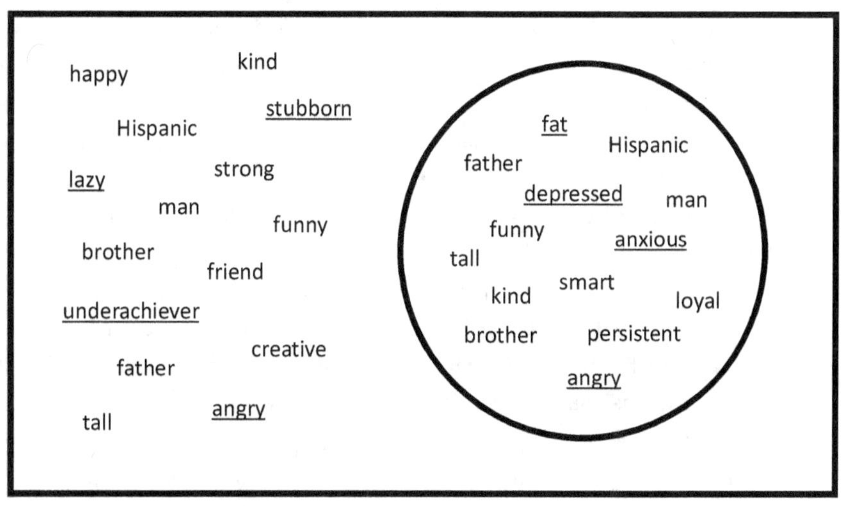

Exercise #2:
Relationship Instruction Manual

A few years ago I was fortunate to have assisted a young client as she successfully escaped a physically and emotionally abusive relationship. After a few more months of therapy working to recover from her trauma she met someone else and wanted to start dating again. As you might expect this created a dilemma.

Her confidence about being in a relationship was deeply wounded. They had been on a couple of dates and she was becoming more attracted to him. But her fears about trusting another person prevented her from getting closer and she was afraid it would drive him away. I reassured her that her fears were understandable given what she had been through. Instead of seeing her fears as a barrier I encouraged her to see them as an asset. I suggested that she write them down so we could process them in our next session.

When she returned she had gone a step further. Instead of simply writing down her fears she had created an instruction manual for being her boyfriend; an actual list of thirty rules and expectations for anyone who wanted to be in her life. It was revolutionary.

After that session she told me her new boyfriend was thrilled. He had always wanted something like this from the women he dated because he was usually frustrated trying to figure it out on his own. My client said it liberated her as well because she felt more confident about asking for exactly what she needed.

The idea of an instruction manual for relationships has value far beyond the context of romantic partnerships. It can be a useful tool for anyone in any relationship including the ones you have with family members, friends, coworkers, and even strangers. The most important first step in having any successful relationship with someone else is coming to terms with your own values. You can't expect anyone else to meet your needs if you can't articulate them yourself.

In the absence of clear values each relationship will have a different set of rules. This will leave you scrambling to adjust to each person's different expectations of you. In the end you will not only find it more and more difficult to keep up, you will eventually lose track of your ability to know yourself in a meaningful way.

In an authentic life you will be more successful by clarifying your own values and applying them to every relationship consistently. This will have a couple of immediate results.

First, you will recognize values that contradict each other. For instance a mother may tolerate abusive language from her son because she wants him to love her. But she would not tolerate the same language from her boss. Why should she make an exception for her son? She either deserves respect from all people or she doesn't. There is no reason to have two different values for how she wants to be treated. Allowing her son to abuse her enables his bad behavior and prevents her from feeling confident about herself.

Second you will identify which relationships support your values and which ones don't. As soon as you begin to apply consistent rules with real consequences people will take notice and let you know where they stand. You may be confronted by those who are uncomfortable with the change. Others may be more passive aggressive and begin to distance themselves from you or criticize you behind your back. This is the investment you must make in order to be more authentic. The return on this investment will be finding the people in your life who can respect your boundaries and deserve your attention.

Third, your emotional workload will dramatically decrease. By streamlining your values you will reduce the amount of effort needed to remember which variation of yourself to be in any given situation. Instead you can focus your energy on actually living by the values that genuinely matter to you. In a short amount of time you will discover that much of the drama that used to cloud your judgement has gone away and you will be able to hear your own inner voice again.

STEP 1: Make a list of the relationships that seem to have the greatest impact on your values. They may be individuals, groups, or larger organizations. In the next column list three conflicts that tend to arise most frequently, or seem to have the greatest influence on the relationship. In the last column list the three most important needs you have to resolve these conflicts.

STEP 2: Use the entries in the last column to create categories for a comprehensive set of rules. Notice how many are similar and which ones are unique to the individual relationship. This may be an indicator that you have extraneous rules that can be blended with other ones for the sake of clarity.

In the example below you can identify some categories related to communication, personal boundaries, and time commitments. So the rules might look like this:

Communication:
- *I expect all communication to be respectful, including my own.*
- *People who communicate with transparency will be given priority over people who don't.*
- *The more specifically you ask me for something the more likely you are to get it.*

Time:
- *I don't owe anyone my time unless I choose to give it.*
- *No one can make a decision about how I spend my time without my consent.*
- *The more consistent you are about your schedule the more likely you are to get some of my time.*
- *If you change your commitment to a schedule I have the right to change my commitment as well.*

Boundaries:
- *I will not allow anyone to discipline my children without consulting me first.*
- *If you have an opinion about me or my actions I will only listen to you tell me about it once.*
- *Empathy goes a long way with me and it will always be rewarded.*
- *I would rather you ask me for help than be mad at me for not offering it.*

STEP 3: As you review your rules look for deeper patterns to help further streamline your values. For instance in the example above there are multiple statements that could be consolidated into a single profound statement that covers a lot of ground.

> ### *I don't owe anyone my time, my money, or my attention unless I choose to give it.*

Take your time going over these rules again and again to make sure they verbalize exactly how you feel about your values and how you will apply them to your life. Be willing to write them down and even share them with people in your life in order to make yourself accountable. As you commit them to memory and put them into practice they will make a real difference in your confidence when conflict arises.

Relationship	What are the most common areas of conflict?	What do I need most from them?
Spouse	• different parenting styles • spending habits • lack of communication	• consult with me first • financial transparency • show some empathy
Mother	• changing the schedule • criticizing my decisions • taking care of her health	• be more consistent • respect my boundaries • ask for help
Book Club	• big time commitment • asking personal questions • changing the schedule	• freedom to set limits • respect my boundaries • be more consistent
School	• community service • discipline issues • schedule changes	• ask for help • respect my boundaries • clear communication
Coworker	• gossip and drama • meeting deadlines • different priorities	• positive communication • respect my boundaries • take responsibility
Daughter	• leaving a mess • talking back • fighting with brother	• take responsibility • positive communication • being respectful

Exercise #3:
Turning Fear Into Values

This exercise is especially effective for helping your emotional immune system process difficult feelings in a meaningful way. The onset of fear can short circuit your rational thinking and lead to unhealthy choices or feelings of doubt. Many see fear as a sign of weakness or as a barrier to becoming their authentic self. By examining the values behind your fear you can see it as an asset rather than a liability.

For this exercise to work you must first recognize that the only reason you are afraid of anything is because you care about it. If you didn't care about anything you wouldn't have anything to be afraid of. This means your fear is a direct result of your values. They can't exist without each other. They are like two sides of the same coin.

In order to keep fear from taking over we can learn to identify the value that causes it, and then develop an action plan to respond when that fear shows up. The following chart can help you practice this strategy and use it on a regular basis to relieve anxieties and help you feel more confident that you can do something about them.

In the following chart are typical examples of fears some clients might work on in a session. In the first example the person might be a student who is under enormous pressure to keep her grades above a certain level. When she takes a deeper look the fear is really about her anxiety about being humiliated. This insight helps her reframe the mindset about how to manage this feeling when it comes up. She might realize she has had a number of achievements to be proud of and already knows how to succeed. If she continues to do those things that make her successful there is every reason to believe it will happen again.

In the second example a person may be afraid to have a difficult conversation about setting boundaries. She is worried her friend may be offended. But instead of being a barrier, her fear may actually be a strength in disguise. It is because of her empathy that she is so sensitive to the needs of her friend, so it will likely be an asset that makes her conversation go well.

In the third example the young man has a persistent anxiety about running out of money and ending up homeless. He may take pride in

being
self-reliant but the deeper concern about being a burden is really about his self-image. The actions he has taken in the past prove that he can be the person he wants to be. He may see this fear as a sign of weakness, but it has motivated him to be the person he wants to be. In this way the fear can serve instead as a reminder of his resilience and authenticity.

STEP 1: In the first column list a few of the fears that seem to hold you back the most or have the greatest impact on your self-image. Think about areas of your life that make you feel stuck or out of control.

STEP 2: Allow yourself to imagine the worst possible consequences of this fear actually happening in your life. This is an important part of embracing your vulnerability and overcoming the anxiety related to this idea in your mind.

STEP 3: Make a brief statement about how a negative outcome effects your sense of self. At this point you are shifting your focus from the imaginary world of anxiety to the reality of how you see yourself in the present and who you want to be.

STEP 4: Do your best to identify a single word or idea to clarify how your identity is defined by your concern. If this is difficult you may need to explore your answer in the second column more deeply. An inability to connect values with fears could be identifying repressed aspects of your personality or conflicting values. It's possible that the value you have in this column is something you don't want to admit about yourself. It might open up other fears that need to be addressed.

STEP 5: The value associated with a fear usually comes from previous experience or observation of others. Think about a time when you faced this fear or a similar situation and how you responded? What sacrifices or efforts did you make in order to uphold your value? Notice that the last two columns are integrated. This is designed to create a link between the actions that have worked for you in the past and choices you can make in the future. As you practice this process you can begin to develop a skill that reframes your fears from limitations into an action plan based on your authentic values.

Fear		Value		Action	
What am I afraid of?	*What is the worst that could happen if my fear came true?*	*This is unacceptable because I am a person who ______.*	*What value is connected to this personality trait?*	*How have I proven this is important to me in the past?*	*When this fear happens I will ______.*
Failing in school	I would feel humiliated.	takes pride in my work	Excellence	• remember my achievements • clearly define success • ask for help	
Conflict with my best friend	We would have a fight and never speak again.	cares about how people feel	Empathy	• listen empathically • be forgiving • express gratitude	
Going broke	I would be homeless	wants to take care of myself	Self-Reliance	• pay my bills on time • save money • plan ahead	

Exercise #4:
Values Game

One of the primary exercises in seeking greater authenticity is clarifying your values and applying them to your life in a practical way. In the real world this can get confusing and a little disorganized. Defining your values requires a lot of trial and error and most of the time some amount of sacrifice. Even though this may be difficult, the end result is a set of priorities that has been tested and streamlined for maximum impact.

This exercise is a game I use with clients to help them practice the thinking that is needed to make decisions about their values in a more non-threatening way. It involves a set of generic values that tend to be common for most adults. They are chosen merely to get the ball rolling and to make it easier to understand the concept. In truth they are arbitrary and can be rewritten to fit your individual needs.

ROUND 1: Choose from the list of twelve values at the top of the worksheet to fill in the blanks of the first column in order of their importance to you. One of the values is a wild card you can use to fill in an additional value of your choice. As you complete this process pay attention to your thoughts about how you make these decisions. Ask yourself the following questions.

- What did you find difficult or easy about prioritizing your values?
- What surprised you about your decisions?
- What criteria did you use to make your decisions?

ROUND 2: In the second column repeat the process of filling in the blanks in order of importance choosing only nine of the values you started with. As you eliminate three of the original values ask yourself a few more questions.

- Which values maintained their status?
- Which values changed their importance?
- How did removing some values effect the ranking of the other values?

ROUND 3: Once again repeat the process in the third column by eliminating three more values for a total of six. Pay attention to the emotional and intellectual experience of making these choices. Ask yourself these questions.

- What thoughts do you have about letting go of certain values?
- What sort of deals do you make with yourself to decide which values to keep?
- Which values have increased their importance from the first round?

ROUND 4: In this final round eliminate all but three of the values. This should give you a very short list of the values you hold dear. As you complete this exercise process the following questions.

- What does it cost you to keep these values at the top of the list?
- How do these values help you live an authentic life?
- What new insights did you gain from this process

Financial Security	Time With Others	Time To Myself	Feeling Loved
Serving Others	Having Nice Things	Having Freedom	Being Creative
Personal Growth	Physical Fitness	Emotional Health	Wild Card

	Round 1	Round 2	Round 3	Round 4
1				
2				
3				
4				
5				
6				
7				
8				
9				
9				
10				
11				
12				

Exercise #5:
Personal Mission Statement

This exercise is one that offers an opportunity to examine your core values in a way that leads to a specific target statement you can use to clarify and verify your progress toward authenticity.

A personal mission statement can be applied to your life as you set daily goals or to guide you in long term planning. It is also helpful as a tool for relationships or in other groups that need to look ahead and stay focused on a particular set of values.

The process begins with a story. Imagine you have lived to be a hundred years old and all of your family and friends have gathered to celebrate your life. Everyone who has been impacted by you has come together to express their appreciation for the way you have made their lives better.

As part of the festivities a dear friend is walking around with a video camera to document the event. In particular she is asking everyone the same question.

How did (*your name here*) make your life better?

Their response will likely include some aspects of your personality, or something you did that stands out as an important contribution to their life. In order to begin this exercise ask yourself… What do you want them to say? After living a full life with countless friends and family you have helped along the way what do you want them to feel about you?

STEP 1:   Make a list of words to describe you or your actions that you want people to remember about you. It might help to fill in the blanks of the following sentences to get you started.

He has always been _______________________.

I could count on her to ___________________.

They helped me learn how to _________________.

The list might look something like this:

kind creative advocate caring empathic talented persistent listener

The list can be as long as you'd like but make a point to notice which items are the most important to you.

STEP 2: Start by writing down these four words:

My mission is to...

Using the list draft a single sentence that includes the most important words needed to represent your purpose in life. You don't have to use all of the words, and you can add ideas as needed. There's no need to worry about making it perfect. It can be done in whatever way works for you as long as you are working towards creating a statement that feels meaningful.

It will help to use action words that define what you do and adjectives that describe how you will do it. As you begin it will probably be a little messy and confusing. Take a look at the list and try to arrange the ideas together in a way that makes sense. You can expect to rewrite it over and over again many times to get it right. If you aren't good at it ask for help from someone who is good with words.

Here is an example of how a personal mission statement using the words above might look:

My mission is to care for others by listening to them and advocating with creativity and persistence.

Remember most of all that this is just a first draft. It will almost certainly need to be rewritten and edited many times over to get it just right. Even after you get it right it might need to change in the future.

STEP 3: Once you get a complete statement take a look at how it lines up with your current situation. Compare it to the areas of your life that get the most attention.

Calendar – How much of your schedule matches up with your mission statement? When you wake up in the morning ask yourself what are you going to do today to make your mission statement come true. When you go to bed make an assessment of how well you lived up to your personal mission statement and what do you want to do better.

Money – What items on your bank statement helped you get closer to living out your mission statement? What items are getting in the way? What will it cost you if you really started to live out your mission statement with integrity? What would be the best return on your investment.

Relationships – Who is your best ally in fulfilling your mission statement? Are there people in your life that discourage you or distract you from reaching this goal? If you told the whole world about your mission statement would you be proud of your efforts or want to keep them a secret?

Each area of life will help you measure how well and how often you are being the person you actually want to be. A personal mission statement is a powerful way to keep you in the right direction toward living up to your authentic values. Even when you fall short of your target you can build confidence knowing you have clear information about what needs to change in order to improve.

I strongly encourage you to print your mission statement and display it proudly in your home or office. Share it with people who can support you. Make a point to review it regularly and change it as needed to serve as a real world reminder of your goal to live an authentic life.

Exercise #6:
Mini-Meditations

Frequently I hear complaints from clients about meditation. It's not unusual for someone to say they can't do it, or it doesn't work for them. When I suggest that it can be very helpful for them to improve resiliency and bolster their coping skills they say they've tried it before, and resist trying it again.

On most things I don't like to push back too much. If you don't want to do something I generally don't want to "make" you do it. But in the case of meditation I feel it's essential to reaching a level of personal awareness that allows you to be clear and present as you seek authenticity. Skipping this practice is such a huge mistake because it is such an effortless way to gain so much benefit.

At the same time I recognize that meditation can be intimidating for those who have met with a sense of failure. There seems to be a lot of pressure in the mainstream culture to be good at it. Feeling inadequate about your meditation skills is reasonable if you don't have a more practical perspective about how to do it. That's why I've looked for ways to demystify the practice of meditation so that it is accessible to people who have failed in the past.

Here's the bottom line… YOU ARE SUPPOSED TO FAIL AT IT. That's the point. Of course you're not good at it. If you were good at it you would already be doing it. That's why it's called a practice. You have to keep doing it in order to find any benefit from it. The best part is that failure is not only part of meditation… it's the point of meditation. It's how you know you're doing it right.

There are a multitude of methods and techniques you can use to practice meditation. So I won't go into describing a particular meditation style. You can pick whichever one that eventually works for you. It's a bit like finding a therapist. You will probably need to try out a few.

If you want to sit with your legs crossed in a temple wearing an orange robe like a monk go right ahead, but that's not really necessary. This is what usually discourages people who don't want to live up to that expectation. Instead I use a much broader definition to help my clients overcome their resistance and anxiety about building a meditation practice.

In general all meditation strategies are targeting the same outcome; to become more aware of your thoughts in order to reach a more stable emotional and physical state. This means you will usually have to do something that makes you think about your own thinking. Whatever technique you choose you will probably be trying to do one thing with your mind and then you will catch yourself doing something else.

For example you might be trying to focus on your breathing and counting in your head as you inhale and exhale. And then you start thinking about the football game yesterday, and then your grocery list, and then your laundry, and then that guy you forgot to email at work. A few seconds might go by, or even minutes, before you remember that you were supposed to be counting your breath. And then you feel like a failure because you forgot to meditate while you were meditating.

Guess what. You're not a failure. That's what you are supposed to do. The practice of meditation is to recognize the contrast between all of those random wandering thoughts and the feeling of present moment thinking that happens immediately after you catch yourself. That dramatic shift of awareness actually causes microscopic changes to the neurons in your brain building new thought patterns and laying a foundation for emotional resiliency.

It's not just about blissing out. It's about adapting the structure of your brain so you can have an alternative to the chaotic, unstructured thinking you normally have throughout the day. Every time you fail at meditation you are spending a few seconds in a new place in your brain. You are developing the ability to recognize the difference between the noise of unfocused thinking and whatever the opposite of that is.

As you practice meditation you are really practicing the skill of catching yourself over and over again. By repeating that experience for weeks, months, and eventually years, the habit of catching yourself will translate into your daily life, helping you become skillful at noticing and taking control of your emotional and physical reactions to people and events that influence you.

Nonetheless, I'm willing to accept that a formal meditation practice might still be intimidating for a lot of people. So I propose an easier way to implement a regular meditation practice. If you're not sure how to begin, or find it hard to schedule specific times for meditation, you can easily incorporate it into your life through **mini-meditations**.

The idea of a mini-meditation is to set the lowest possible goal you can set and still get results. For some people trying to meditate for even five minutes a day is an unrealistic expectation. So I suggest meditating for only five seconds. And to make it easier you don't even have to schedule a time. A mini-meditation is a brief moment of reflection connected to your regular activities without having to plan ahead or interfere with your day.

Humans are creatures of habit who repeat patterns of behavior all the time without noticing. When we wake up we usually follow a certain path from our bed through the rest of our day ending up back where we started. We do things a certain way, put things in a specific place, and visit particular locations with regularity, all without recognizing how familiar and comforting they are. With a mini-meditation you can choose to attach a five second moment of awareness to just a few of these habits that you complete on a regular basis.

IDEA #1: Objects – You can attach a mini-meditation to certain objects that you use consistently. It might be something on your desk, or something you wear, or even a credit card you use to buy things. Then uncover the meaning you may have unconsciously attached to that object and how it impacts your ability to be authentic.

For instance, you likely put your keys in the same place when you come home at the end of the day. As you put them where they belong observe a five second moment of gratitude for all the things they keep secure for you. You don't have to spend a long time on it. Just do a quick check in and your meditation is done.

IDEA #2: Transitions – Another idea for creating mini-meditations are moments of transition from one activity to another. Let these events remind you to accept change as part of growth. You can choose a doorway or entrance to a building you often pass through as a reminder to be authentic in each new place. In the evening when you notice the street lights flicker on ask yourself what new ideas you learned today.

When you get into your car ready to drive away, take a deep breath as you place your hand on the gear shift and be in the moment. For a few seconds be still and appreciate the contrast between coming and going. Are you feeling hurried and worried, or are you calm and comfortable? Make a quick assessment of your mental state and then go on about your business. Meditation accomplished. And you will probably drive safer as a result.

IDEA #3: Rituals – There are lots of things you do each day that feel like mindless chores that can be used instead as opportunities for mindfulness. Take a look at your daily rituals and add a small mini-meditation to increase their meaning and promote self-awareness. Before you eat make a point to smell your food and imagine how each ingredient contributes to the flavor of your meal. Whenever you send an email take a second before you hit send to be grateful for technology.

Wait a few seconds at the end of every shower as you stand there letting the water drip off your body and down the drain. In that moment give yourself a chance to be present and work on self-acceptance. Remind yourself that even when you feel exposed and vulnerable, every day is a new opportunity to wash away all of your negative inner thoughts and pledge to be fully authentic. It's a powerful meditation that only takes a moment.

As you continue to practice these mini-meditations you will not only develop a few new habits, it will change how you see yourself completely. Meditation won't just be something you do. It will become part of a larger evolution in who you are. Learning how to watch your thoughts and allow them to ebb and flow will make it easier to accept yourself more fully, and feel more confident about your values and purpose.

Exercise #7:
Finding Features In Your Flaws

One of the most basic skills in marketing is being able to list the features and benefits of a product. If you are selling anything from a kitchen utensil to a car, or even a new idea, you will be more effective at motivating buyers if you describe clearly the particular aspects of the thing you are trying to sell and how it will make their lives better.

Making a list of your own features and benefits would be a useful exercise to help increase authenticity. What are the aspects of your personality that improve your life and the lives of others around you? How can others benefit from what you have to offer? In my experience however, when I have asked clients to make this list they tend to be far better at listing their flaws instead.

From a cultural perspective we have been conditioned to fixate on our insecurities. People without deficiencies cannot easily be convinced to want more stuff. So we are living in an economy that thrives on perpetuating a pervasive flaw-based culture.

While we celebrate people who stand out, we face enormous pressure to conform. We may be rewarded for being special at the same time that we feel punished for being different. It's hard to know which aspects of our personality are acceptable and which attributes might be stigmatized.

This leaves us with a dilemma. If we are expected to work on our flaws in order to become socially acceptable, we inadvertently reinforce them by making them our focus. Such anxiety about finding and fixing flaws trains our brain to identify weaknesses much more than finding strengths.

In order to increase authenticity it is best to question the idea that flaws and features are opposite of one another, and to examine them on a spectrum instead. This exercise is designed to help you recognize that the aspects of your personality are neither good or bad. How they are expressed makes a big difference in their impact on your life.

Parts of your personality that are generally considered positive can become distorted and destructive when taken to the extreme. Kindness may be seen as a strength in moderation but too much kindness can lead to codependency or even victimization. People with persistence can overcome challenges admirably but too much persistence can unwittingly add to those challenges and cloud good judgement.

In the same way, any aspect of your personality that seems inherently negative can be moderated in a way that yields positive results. If you struggle with extreme anger you may try to eliminate that feeling completely. But doing this might lead you to be dangerously passive or indifferent instead. A reasonable amount of justified anger may be helpful in motivating you to protect yourself without losing control.

Any personality trait that is expressed to the extreme will almost always lead to unpleasant outcomes. You may be driven to compensate for this imbalance by swinging to the other extreme, acting in a way that is equally detrimental. In order to reach the sweet spot in the middle you need to identify a moderate expression of each extreme to transform them into a beneficial feature.

With practice you can begin to appreciate the personality traits you usually find troublesome as potentially favorable. When you recognize that your perceived flaws on both extremes are not only useful but necessary to balance each other out, your new goal is to recalibrate them to help you function at your best.

STEP 1: In the first column of the chart begin by listing a personality trait that you feel leads to negative outcomes in your life. In general it works best if this is an adjective or noun that describes a typical behavior or emotional response. For instance you might put "too sensitive" or choose "hypersensitive" to be more precise.

STEP 2: In the far right column enter a word that describes the extreme opposite of the original attribute. This may be different for each person. As in the example one person may see the opposite of anger as apathy, while another might see it as helplessness. There is no one right answer other than the one that best expresses your own understanding of yourself.

STEP 3: Next to each attribute, find another word that is less extreme and represents a level of expression that is milder or neutral. Imagine describing the extreme attribute as a lighter version of itself. Do this for both ends of the spectrum looking for a word that represents a healthier balance between the two.

STEP 4: In the middle column invent a descriptive phrase that seems like a reasonable blend between the two moderate words on either side. It might help to make one an adjective and the other a noun so they sound like a marketing label. Remember this entire process is a way to clarify a feature of your personality that is beneficial to yourself and others.

FLAW		FEATURE		FLAW
Anger	Awareness	Alert Engagement	Acceptance	Helplessness
Empathy	Compassion	Supportive Boundaries	Detachment	Apathy
Cynicism	Caution	Pragmatic Discernment	Optimism	Idealism
Perfectionism	Excellence	Measured Achievement	Restraint	Negligence

After you've completed this process for a few of your attributes look at the middle column and consider how these choices can support your values when you feel out of balance. Recognize that when you feel overwhelmed by aspects of your personality that make you feel ashamed or frustrated, you now have a different choice about how to react. What used to feel like a painful flaw is really a valuable part of you that can be adjusted for maximum benefit.

When you feel angry or helpless choose to practice alert engagement for the better results. Unchecked empathy can lead to problems but you can still be supportive if you set healthy boundaries. Cynicism and perfectionism are weaknesses that can be turned into strengths by blending them with the opposite extreme.

As you follow the steps think about how you tend to view personality traits as all or nothing attributes and learn to shift your thinking toward a more balanced perspective about yourself. Because it is primarily a verbal exercise it might help to have a thesaurus handy to help pick words that fit what you are trying to communicate.

Take your time and be willing to adapt your answers as you look for clarity. It also makes for a great discussion starter with friends who know you well and can give honest (hopefully constructive) feedback to help you see yourself more clearly.

RESOURCES

Here is a list of materials that have been essential in planting and nurturing the ideas presented in this book. As I said in the introduction, this book is intentionally concise in order to leave room for lots of questions. If you really want to get the most out of this book take the time to research and explore these resources and see where they take you. The best way to do this is by simply being curious and letting your intuition guide you.

I have included specific books that I think will be a good place to start because they helped me think of new ideas and motivated me to ask endless questions. I've also included some general concepts that you can research to build a critical body of knowledge about mental health in order to continue working on yourself and support others who come into your life.

Authentic Values

The Book; on the taboo against knowing who you are – Alan Watts
His status as a cultural icon, educator, and speaker from previous generations makes him a vital inspiration for those eager to learn more about Eastern and Western philosophy. He has written many books and recorded countless hours of lectures explaining the human experience with clever and profound wisdom. I would consider this the masterpiece of his collection. If you only read one book from this author this is it.

Think Like a Freak – Stephen Dubner & Steven Levitt
As hosts of the podcast Freakonomics they have been a huge influence on my ability to examine mental health from a broader perspective. This book is useful in helping ask better questions and think like a child in order to make practical decisions about how to live with integrity.

Collaborative Therapy is an approach to therapy more than a specific set of techniques. As a postmodern strategy for mental health it equalizes the relationship between therapist and client by questioning some core assumptions that often interfere with authentic work.

Authentic Emotions

The Body Keeps The Score – Bessel Van der Kolk & Sean Pratt

This comprehensive resource provides detailed information about the physical impact of severe emotional distress. It offers insight into the causes and treatments of trauma and deep emotional wounds caused by events in the world and at home.

The Dance of Anger – Harriet Lerner

Written as a guidebook for women working to free themselves from the cultural constraints of the era, many have found it to be a practical examination of hidden relationship patterns that lead to poor self-image and even mental illness. These ideas are integral to becoming more accepting and appreciative of your negative emotions.

The Search Institute

With research into the lives of millions of youth throughout the world this organization has designed a comprehensive program to understand and promote the development of resiliency for children and teens. Their work in communities in schools relies on a wealth of resources to support the work of professionals and volunteers dedicated to helping youth. www.search-institute.org

Authentic Intentions

Daring Greatly – Brene' Brown

As a bestselling author and speaker she has quickly become an international advocate for authentic living through her research about shame and vulnerability. Her books and presentations have revolutionized the field of mental health and accentuated the need for courage and transparency in public and private life.

Acceptance and Commitment Therapy (ACT) is a treatment strategy that helps clients recognize inflexible thinking that leads to severe emotional distress. Through therapy and mindfulness practices clients work to replace problematic beliefs with a commitment to take positive action. This integrates well with the pathway through disillusionment and can be a solid plan to use in therapy.

Authentic Relationships

Codependent No More – Melody Beattie

This inspirational classic has made a culture changing impact on the field of mental health by examining the idea of codependency and how it can hinder the well-being of so many good intentioned people trapped in unhealthy relationships. It can be a clear and simple call for anyone striving to become more authentic amidst fears of conflict and shame.

The Shadow Effect – Debbie Ford

An essential exploration of the destructive impact felt from unresolved inner conflict and ways to use these negative aspects of ourselves to gain strength and grow towards a more authentic identity.

Jungian Psychology represents a classical approach to psychotherapy driven by the work of Carl Jung. Much of our modern understanding of mental health finds it roots in his monumental exploration into the psyche and the shadow aspect of self. Although his prolific work may be difficult to fully comprehend and somewhat perplexing, I think any amount of exposure to his ideas can be beneficial to your journey toward self-awareness.

Authentic Living

Orbiting The Giant Hairball – Gordon Mackenzie

This book was an important milestone in giving myself permission to pursue an authentic life with creativity and integrity. It convinced me that humor was not only acceptable but essential to telling stories and motivating others. The author found himself in a predicament working at Hallmark cards striving to retain his creativity in a corporate world. This crisis led him to create the now famous Shoebox collection and transform the industry forever. His energetic and playful style is inspiring and empowering.

Free To Learn – Peter Gray

As a leading psychologist and educator he has become an important advocate in the field of education and children's rights. This book is used by many in the alternative education movement to elevate the status of children by giving them the freedom to determine their own direction in their education. Although it is primarily targeted at the needs of children many of its ideas are universal to humans of all ages and can be used to expand and possibly heal adults with unsatisfying and traumatic childhoods.

Tao; The Watercourse Way – Alan Watts

Many years ago this book introduced me to a new way of thinking about the purpose of suffering and finding meaning in life. With poetic elegance he describes the role of water as a source of inspiration for anyone willing to allow life to guide them toward authenticity.

ACKNOWLEGEMENTS

This book could not exist without the courage and authenticity of the people I have been honored to serve throughout the years. I owe an enormous debt to all of you who have trusted me with your honesty and vulnerability. I have learned a great deal from you as we have worked together to find innovative approaches to meeting life's challenges with integrity.

I want to thank my wife and best friend Karen who inspires me and reminds me to give myself permission to do whatever I want. I also want to thank my two sons who remind me to be playful and not take things too seriously.

I deeply appreciate my friend and hero Tony who makes me feel like anything is possible and to stay true to my calling even when things get tough. You are a sacred blessing, miracle, and gift.

I have enormous gratitude for the collaboration of so many friends and colleagues who have assisted with the editing and quality of this book. Each and every comment, question, and observation has been treasured and received with diligence. My hope is that you can join me in seeing your contribution extend to the many lives who will benefit from this effort.

Finally, I extend sincere admiration to all of my fellow therapists who do a job that is frankly a little weird. You help me keep believing that people can actually make a living and still change the world at the same time.

ABOUT THE AUTHOR

Dave Waxler is a husband and father who lives in Texas. He has a Master's Degree in Counseling from Sam Houston State University and works in private practice as a Licensed Professional Counselor.

With over a decade of experience in mental health he has worked at a non-profit organization serving at-risk youth, consulted with local schools, and counseled clients of all ages in individual, family and couples therapy.

His presentations at professional conferences encourage other mental health professionals to practice with authenticity and courage. As an author and speaker he offers a uniquely fun and practical approach to mental health and inspiration for those striving to live a more meaningful and authentic life.

To learn about more opportunities to work with him visit

www.newclaritymedia.com

GET CONNECTED

This book is only the beginning.

It was written as an introduction to new ideas and designed to promote further learning and discussion.

Visit our website to:

- participate in the public forum
- access information and resources
- learn about upcoming events
- discuss topics with the author
- share stories about living an authentic life

Join the community at:

www.clearandpresent.net